Quick Lessons for the Real World

What they don't teach you in school

by

Timothy Witt

Contents

ACKNOWLEDGEMENTS   8

INTRODUCTION   9

QUICK LESSONS FOR HANDLING MONEY   11

QUICK LESSON 1: The importance of having a budget   12

QUICK LESSON 2: The importance of managing your money   16

QUICK LESSON 3: How to save money   19

QUICK LESSON 4: How to budget for bills   22

QUICK LESSON 5: What is a credit rating and why is it important?   24

QUICK LESSON 6: Good debt and bad debt   26

QUICK LESSON 7: Budgeting for a wedding   29

QUICK LESSON 8: How to maximise your pension/superannuation fund   31

QUICK LESSON 9: International money transfer accounts   33

QUICK LESSONS FOR THE BUSINESS WORLD   35

QUICK LESSON 10: The basics of how business works in the world we live in   36

QUICK LESSON 11: The benefits of networking   38

QUICK LESSON 12: The importance of a curriculum vitae   40

QUICK LESSON 13: Interviewing   43

QUICK LESSON 14: How to find a job   45

QUICK LESSON 15: Get a job you can enjoy some days and tolerate on other days   47

QUICK LESSON 16: The importance of being a team player   49

QUICK LESSON 17: Customer-focused businesses are much more likely to succeed   51

QUICK LESSON 18: What is cash flow and why is it important?   53

QUICK LESSON 19: Always look after your supply chain   55

QUICK LESSON 20: Always move with the times and develop with economic conditions   57

QUICK LESSON 21: Learn to take and accept negative feedback   59

QUICK LESSON 22: How to negotiate   61

QUICK LESSON 23: The importance of productivity   63

QUICK LESSON 24: How to write an effective email   65

QUICK LESSON 25: How to see the big picture   67

QUICK LESSON 26: Meeting efficiency   69

QUICK LESSON 27: How to problem solve in the workplace   72

QUICK LESSONS ON PROPERTY AND REAL ESTATE   74

QUICK LESSON 28: Saving for a house deposit   75

QUICK LESSON 29: What is property equity and why is it important? 77

QUICK LESSON 30: Ways to add value to your property   79

QUICK LESSON 31: What is remortgaging and what are the benefits? 82

QUICK LESSON 32: What is rental yield and why is it important?   84

QUICK LESSON 33: Buy property from motivated sellers   86

QUICK LESSONS ON GOVERNMENTS AND THE ECONOMY   88

QUICK LESSON 34: Basics of how the government works   89

QUICK LESSON 35: What is globalisation?   91

QUICK LESSON 36: Basics of left-wing and right-wing politics   93

QUICK LESSON 37: How to Vote   95

QUICK LESSON 38: The rise of nationalism   97

QUICK LESSON 39: Basics of how the tax system works   99

QUICK LESSON 40: Completing a tax return   101

QUICK LESSON 41: How international currency exchange rates are determined   103

QUICK LESSONS ON GENERAL LIFE SKILLS   105

QUICK LESSON 42: The importance of emotional intelligence   106

QUICK LESSON 43: Have a plan and set goals   108

QUICK LESSON 44: Dating and relationships   110

QUICK LESSON 45: The importance of sport   112

QUICK LESSON 46: The importance of travel   114

QUICK LESSON 47: The importance of insurance   116

QUICK LESSON 48: The importance of family   119

QUICK LESSON 49: Grades in school aren't 'that' important 121

QUICK LESSON 50: The positives and negatives of alcohol consumption 123

QUICK LESSON 51: The importance of learning about 'irrelevant' information at school 125

QUICK LESSONS ON LIFE SKILLS FOR YOURSELF 127

QUICK LESSON 52: Always be personable with people 128

QUICK LESSON 53: Have multiple income streams 130

QUICK LESSON 54: The importance of time management 132

QUICK LESSON 55: The importance of life balance 134

QUICK LESSON 56: The importance of to-do lists 136

QUICK LESSON 57: Prioritising tasks 138

QUICK LESSON 58: The importance of self-acceptance 140

QUICK LESSON 59: The importance of getting out of your comfort zone 142

QUICK LESSON 60: Learning from failure 144

QUICK LESSON 61: Surround yourself with positive, like-minded people 146

QUICK LESSON 62: Nothing good happens after 2 a.m. 148

QUICK LESSON 63: First aid 150

QUICK LESSON 64: Always look after your belongings 152

QUICK LESSON 65: Importance of putting life into perspective sometimes 154

Acknowledgements

I would like to thank my fiancée Amy for giving me the time in our busy lives to be able to write this book.

I would also like to thank my parents for teaching many life lessons throughout my life.

Introduction

I am a 30-year-old Australian-born and raised who currently resides and works in the United Kingdom as a project manager in the building industry. Ever since I completed my secondary education and to a certain extent my tertiary education, I have learnt various life skills and lessons for my working life and day-to-day life that I really wish I had learnt at a much younger age. These lessons and skills are helpful in what is referred to commonly as the real world post-secondary and tertiary education. I could quite easily recite the periodic table and I knew how to solve numerous algebraic equations; however, I did not know basic life skills, such as how to manage my own money properly or how to lodge a tax return.

As time goes by, I realise how little of what I learnt at school and during my younger years I actually use in day-to-day life. The inspiration and reasoning for writing this book is so that you can learn some of these skills or at least have a basic understanding to build upon. Some of these life lessons and skills may be very basic to some, but they are needed for general day-to-day life and useful to learn in our youthful years. The age range for most of the lessons is from 15 to 25 years.

Just to be clear, this is not a negative view of the education system or the teachers who work in it – especially as my fiancée is a teacher! I am simply trying to fill the gaps of critical items that generally do not fit into mainstream curriculums and include some of the life experiences I have encountered along the way.

This book could also be read by all ages and parents of children who are in their adolescent years, as many aspects may not be specifically taught at school. Please research any of the topics discussed in more detail once you have completed reading. If you would like to learn about any of the quick lessons included, please ask your parents, teachers, friends and relatives who may be able to give you the advice you need.

Hopefully, this book can inspire and motivate you to gain an in-depth knowledge of the skills required for the real world we live in!

QUICK LESSONS FOR HANDLING MONEY

Something I was never really taught in my younger years was how to handle and manage my own money. This is one of the most important skills to help you throughout your entire life. In this section of the book, I will share with you how to manage and save money while also living a balanced life. I could recite to you trigonometric functions, but I could not keep track of the money I was spending, which is a much more important life skill!

QUICK LESSON 1: The importance of having a budget

It is a simple fact that you will not save any money if you spend more than you earn over a period of time. If you are not saving money on a regular basis, you may not be able to live comfortably and there won't be enough for big-ticket items such as a holiday or a new car. Also, building up savings to use for a house deposit, for example, won't be a possibility. How can you manage your spending in a way that ensures you spend less money? You guessed it, have a budget in place and then manage your money against your budget.

I was not specifically taught by anyone to have a weekly/monthly budget, so I self-taught myself the simple art of putting together a basic weekly/monthly budget over a few years, and then it took me even longer to work out how to manage my expenditure against this budget.

Here is a simple way to create a budget:

Step 1) Write down your outgoings over a weekly/monthly period. This would include items such as rental payment, mortgage repayment, cable TV connection, broadband connection and car insurance, which are all fixed/set expenditure. Also list your ongoing expenditure, which includes utility bills and mobile phone bills where the exact costs are not known until each bill is received, so (fairly accurate) estimates will have to be used.

Step 2) Estimate the remaining expenditure you can comfortably live on each week. This may include outgoings such as car petrol, dining out, drinking out, birthday and Christmas presents, football tickets, etc. These costs will obviously fluctuate, but the budget is your best guess at your approximate expenditure to forecast a savings plan. As an example, you will not be buying birthday presents on a weekly basis, but you should know approximately how much you would like to spend on presents throughout the year. These figures should be realistic and achievable as there is no real reason to include figures that will never be manageable.

Step 3) Estimate of the amount of money you would like to save on a weekly basis. I recommend that you include an allowance for short-term savings that could be used to save for a holiday, as an example, and long-term savings to put aside in a separate account for a 'rainy day' cash buffer or, even better, a deposit for a house.

Below is an example of a weekly budget. The totals should add up to your income after tax. The monthly costs are the weekly costs x 4.33 to average out the number of days in each month.

Weekly Budget	
Rent	£87.00
Bills	£31.00
Groceries	£40.00
Train/Tram	£28.50
Saving short-term holidays	£75.00
Saving long term	£126.67
Lunches	£25.00
Petrol	£25.00
Car insurance	£19.23
Entertainment	£100.00
Other/presents, etc.	£47.00
Mortgage costs	£40.00
Gym membership	£4.60
Total	£649.00

Monthly Budget	
Rent	£377.00
Bills	£134.23
Groceries	£173.20
Train/Tram	£123.40
Saving short-term holidays	£325.00
Saving long term	£548.48
Lunches	£108.25
Petrol	£108.25
Car insurance	£83.27
Entertainment	£433.33
Other/presents, etc.	£203.51
Mortgage costs	£173.20
Gym membership	£19.92
Total	£2,811.04

Obviously the above example shows a general budget and this needs to be altered to suit the individual specifics relevant to you. You are never too young or old to put a budget in place. If you are under 18 years old and have a budget, it might even help your parents save money because you will not be asking them for money…

IF YOU ARE NOT CONSISTENTLY SAVING MONEY, YOU MAY NOT HAVE ENOUGH TO LIVE COMFORTABLY AND YOU MAY NOT BE ABLE TO AFFORD A HOLIDAY, A NEW CAR OR A HOUSE DEPOSIT

QUICK LESSON 2: The importance of managing your money

Now you know how to put a basic budget in place, you need to know how to manage your money against this budget to determine if you can realistically save money in the short and long term. Through managing your money against your budget, you will also determine how accurate or realistic your budget actually is. By overseeing your incomings and outgoings, you can update your weekly/monthly budget to reflect your actual expenditure and savings that are being achieved.

In my opinion, the best way to manage your budget is firstly by spending your money with the budget in mind in a general sense, and secondly by recording all your expenditure against the budget you have set. Yes, I mean writing down and recording all your expenditure. I know the second item sounds like a lot of work, but it should only take a few minutes each day to list everything you have spent. By recording your expenditure, it will make you think about what you are spending your money on; therefore, helping you to save money for example the cost of regularly buying takeaway coffee would add up in the long run and you may not realise until you see the costs written down and added up. Below is an example of how to record your expenditure to determine how much money you are spending and saving on a weekly basis.

12 Dec	13 Dec	14 Dec	15 Dec	16 Dec	17 Dec	18 Dec
Monday	Tuesday	Wednesday	Thursday	Friday	Saturday	Sunday
Lunch - £3.60	Lunch - £5.50	Lunch - £4.50	Lunch - £4.79	Groceries - £25	Car insurance - £18	Power Bill - £100
Christmas Present Dad - £42	Tram to work - £5.70	Tram to work - £5.70	Tram to work - £5.70	Lunch - £4.99	Mortgage costs- £40	Panto ticket - £15
Christmas Present Mum - £19.80					Sky Bill - £6	Food & drinks - £35
					Dinner & drinks outs - £61	
					Petrol - £60	
£65.40	£11.20	£10.20	£10.49	£29.99	£185.00	£150
					Total spent	£462.28
					Total spent inc. rent	£549.28
Total saving for week (weekly salary after tax (£710)– total spent inc. rent (£549.28))						£160.72

If recording all your expenditure as detailed above is too time-consuming, you could simply record your bank account totals on a monthly basis to see how much you spend against your set budget. This basic technique is a good way of showing how much money is being spent per month, but it will not give you as much information as recording all your expenditure and may not be as successful for achieving your saving goals.

Below is a simple example showing how to record monthly spending by recording your bank account totals on the same day each month.

	Bank Account Totals	Money Spent	Money Saved
01/12/2016	£15,243.00	£0	£0
01/01/2017	£15,879.00	£2,166.00	£636.00
01/02/2017	£16,456.00	£2,225.00	£577.00
01/03/2017	£17,037.00	£2,221.00	£581.00
01/04/2017	£17,667.00	£2,172.00	£630.00

I am not advocating being 'cheap' with your money or to be the boring one who never goes out for a meal/drink simply because you are saving money (refer to the Quick Lesson 55 on life balance). My suggestion is to set a realistic budget for 'entertainment' to cover what you feel you can spend to have a balanced life. Also, do not beat yourself up about overspending or not spending much money on occasions as this will happen for various reasons and some of these will be unforeseen, which is a part of life to a certain extent.

By having a budget in place and then managing your expenditure against that budget, you should be on the road to saving money and making good choices with your expenditure, which in the long run will hopefully make for a happy life with your finances generally.

MY SUGGESTION IS TO SET A REALISTIC BUDGET FOR 'ENTERTAINMENT' TO COVER WHAT YOU FEEL YOU CAN SPEND TO HAVE A BALANCED LIFE

QUICK LESSON 3: How to save money

There are a lot of suggestions and tips on how to save money. You could google this topic right now and I'm sure you could find literally millions of suggestions. In this quick lesson, I will focus on the overall mindset of saving money rather than individual detailed methodologies.

My basic lesson on how to save money is to spend less than you earn over a period of time on a consistent basis but also live a well-balanced life. Live within your means and use your gut instinct to make decisions about your expenditure based on the information that you have now included in your weekly/monthly budget.

Make sure you set saving goals that will suit your lifestyle. Keep in mind that if you are not saving at least 20% of your income, you may struggle to save enough money for a new car, a deposit to get on the housing ladder or to go travelling, etc. If you do not want to save enough money for these types of expenditure, then set your budget based on that lifestyle.

If you are spending more money than you are budgeting for, prioritise your spending based on the lifestyle you would like. So, if travelling abroad is more important than having a full subscription to Netflix, you might want to look at cancelling that subscription.

My top three money-saving tips:

1. Record and monitor all your expenditure against the weekly/monthly budget you have set.

2. Look at your fixed costs included in your weekly/monthly budget, determine whether you need these items and then continually look for a better deal. For example, I am sure you could always get a better deal for your car insurance and cable TV package if you shopped around and negotiated.

3. In the months that you do not meet your savings budget, look through your expenditure recorded and determine why this is the case and whether you have spent money on items that were not necessary, i.e. did not add value to your lifestyle. Did buying a round of drinks for 20 people at the bar add to your lifestyle? Can you even remember buying that round of drinks? Hopefully you understand this point.

Another basic guideline I have learnt is applying the 50-30-20 principle. This guideline includes spending 50% of your income on committed expenses, which might include items such as mortgage repayment, utility bills and food. The 30% is on items that are not necessities, such as dinner out, going to the movies and going out for drinks. The final 20% should go into a savings account.

> **MY BASIC LESSON ON HOW TO SAVE MONEY IS TO SPEND LESS THAN YOU EARN OVER A PERIOD OF TIME ON A CONSISTENT BASIS BUT ALSO LIVE A WELL-BALANCED LIFE**

QUICK LESSON 4: How to budget for bills

Once you are living in your property or rented accommodation, bills are something you will never be able to escape as they are a factor of everyday adult life. Paying bills, or more importantly budgeting for bills, is not something I learnt until living away from home when I was in my twenties. Paying bills is quite simple and self-explanatory, and it can usually be completed using the internet or over the phone with a debit or credit card. The difficult skill is budgeting for bills and knowing how much they will cost, which is an area many adults struggle with throughout periods of their life.

Basic household bills generally include electricity, water, gas, council tax and phone. Then there are other household bills that could include items such as broadband, cable, TV licence, insurances, car finance payments, magazine subscriptions, book subscriptions, wine club subscriptions, etc. For the purpose of this quick lesson, I will stick to budget setting for utility bills. So how much should these cost? The cost of these bills depends on a few factors, so I will use a basic average cost experienced within the United Kingdom.

- Council tax rates in the UK can be found on the internet. For example, we pay £1,019 a year. The council tax rates will vary depending on what band category your property falls under and the council area that you are located in.

- Electricity bills will obviously vary depending on the size of the property and the consumption; however, an average in the UK would be approximately £350 per person per year for a 1-2 bed flat

- Water bills again will vary depending on the size of the property and consumption, but the UK average is approximately £200 per property per year.

- Gas bills, not always applicable if you live in a flat or apartment, will vary depending on the size of the property, the consumption and also the time of year with regards to heating; however, the UK average is approximately £4000 per person per year for a 1-2 bed flat.

Please search online for accurate estimates of how much utility bills will cost in your area, and then use this information in your weekly/monthly budget you are now using from Quick Lesson 1. By working to this budget, you should hopefully never be in a situation where you won't have enough money to pay these bills on time. This is important as it can influence your overall credit rating, which I discuss in Quick Lesson 5.

> **THE DIFFICULT SKILL IS BUDGETING FOR BILLS AND KNOWING HOW MUCH THEY SHOULD COST**

QUICK LESSON 5: What is a credit rating and why is it important?

I am sure I was not taught this topic during my educational studies, but it can be very important throughout anyone's adult life because it will generally affect the type of monetary loans and mortgages available to you.

A credit rating is an estimate of the ability of a person or organisation to fulfil commercial/financial commitments based upon the previous dealings of that person or organisation. The credit rating is then used by financial institutions to determine if you qualify for a money loan, mortgage, credit card or other service, such as certain insurances and even mobile phone contracts. Bank lenders use different models to calculate your credit score, which then represents your credit history. This helps to indicate the type of borrower you are and the type of loan that would be available to you.

The higher your credit score and rating, the lower you are a risk in the eyes of lending institutions. Listed below are a few factors that influence your credit rating as well as advice on how to improve your credit score.

Basic factors that may affect your credit score and rating:

1. History of credit card repayments

2. Repayment history for loans, utility bills and other monthly bills/services

3. Amount of money owed already (student loan, car loan, etc.)

4. How often you move

5. Being on the electoral roll

Basic advice that may assist in boosting a higher credit score and rating:

1. Obtain a credit card and make the monthly payments so you can prove that you have a repayment history

2. Never default on credit card repayments

3. Make sure you are registered to vote, as this will provide the bank and financial institutions with proof of your address

4. Living in an address for at least three years helps to improve your credit score

5. Link with a partner financially by setting up a shared bank account, mortgage, etc.

6. Make sure you're always on the electoral roll

THE HIGHER YOUR CREDIT SCORE AND RATING, THE LOWER YOU ARE A RISK IN THE EYES OF LENDING INSTITUTIONS

QUICK LESSON 6: Good debt and bad debt

Most people generally perceive monetary debt as a negative for your financial situation and that debts should be avoided at all costs. I agree with this for 'bad debt'. However, there is of course debt that is good, especially in the long term.

I would consider any type of debt that is an investment and provides an increased monetary return as being 'good debt'. Essentially, the more of this type of debt the better because you will eventually be in a better financial situation as a result. Some examples of what could be considered as good debts are detailed below.

1. Mortgage – You will have to take out a mortgage loan to buy a house/flat, which will result in having a large amount of debt. Generally (depending on the area where you buy and economic conditions), this property should appreciate (increase) in value over time and you will make a monetary return on your investment.

2. Debt to start up a business – You might have to take out a loan if you want to start your own business. If your business is then successful and profitable, this would be a good debt because you are making a monetary return from the business.

3. Student loan – Most people will have to take out a student loan to study at university or any other tertiary institutions. Although you will not necessarily receive a direct monetary return from this debt, it will of course help you to gain qualifications to enable you to earn money in the future.

On the contrary, bad debt can occur from monetary loans that do not provide an increase in value over time or any kind of monetary return on your investment. Some examples of bad debt are listed below.

1. Loan for a car purchase – Most cars don't usually increase in value overtime (unless it is a classic car, for example), so they are generally not a solid monetary investment. Not only will you be in debt if you take out a loan for a car, but you will be paying interest on the loan for an item that is usually decreasing in value over time. My suggestion is to buy a car you can comfortably afford with the money you have saved.

2. Loan for a holiday – Although I agree that holidays are important and travel is one of the best things you can

do in life, taking out a loan or debt to pay for it is not a good idea financially. Once you have been on your holiday, there is no further monetary return. My suggestion is to go on holidays you can comfortably afford with money you have saved to avoid this type of debt.

3. Unmanageable credit card debt – A small amount of this type of debt is fine and actually helps your credit rating, but large credit card debt can result in large repayments as well as being charged additional interest on the debt you owe.

I WOULD CONSIDER ANY TYPE OF DEBT THAT IS AN INVESTMENT AND PROVIDES AN INCREASED MONETARY RETURN AS BEING 'GOOD DEBT'

QUICK LESSON 7: Budgeting for a wedding

If you intend to get married, which is approximately 80% of the population in the UK and Australia, you will need to put a budget in place and start a savings plan. I read that the average cost for a wedding in the UK is around £20,000, which gives you an idea of the overall cost associated. This may explain why many people marry later in life than previous generations. I am 30 years old as I write this book and I'm engaged to be married after my 31st birthday, as an example. I understand that many parents contribute towards the expense of a wedding, but this should not be relied upon or even expected as this would be a bonus.

There is no need to rush into a lifelong commitment; everyone is different depending on each individual situation. Obviously, the timing of a marriage will depend on the type of relationship you are in (if you are in a relationship at all) and what your priorities are in life. Personally, I always wanted to have a career in place and go travelling before I settled down, so there are no set guidelines on how you wish to live your life. You will just need to make sure that you and your partner are on the same page with regards to your plans for the future.

If you are a male, there is generally a fairly large initial cost for the engagement ring. This cost is completely discretional and everyone will need to set their own budget depending on individual circumstances. Just remember when you are looking for an engagement ring that your partner should be wearing it for the rest of their life and that the average cost is around £3,300. Further to this, I suggest looking online for the specifics on the '4 Cs of diamond rings' and ask advice from a trustworthy friend!

THE AVERAGE COST FOR A WEDDING IN THE UK IS AROUND £20,000, WHICH GIVES YOU AN IDEA OF THE OVERALL COST ASSOCIATED

QUICK LESSON 8: How to maximise your pension/superannuation fund

Pension/superannuation funds are investment accounts into which you and/or your employer contribute money throughout your working life to then access as your income once you have retired, which at the time of publication of this book is now 63 years old for women and 65 years old for men. Most people don't know what is happening to their pension/superannuation funds until they are close to retirement. Don't you think it would be a good idea to maximise the return on your pension fund early in your working life so you can feel the benefits once you have retired?

I believe the best way to maximise your pension/superannuation fund in the United Kingdom and Australia is simply to pay more into it. Not just because you are putting more money away for retirement, but because of the tax relief associated with pension payments. For example, if you are a high-income earner with a yearly salary of over £150,000, you should be paying tax on approximately 50% of your income. If you increase your pension payments, then the money you put away for your pension fund will qualify for tax relief at your marginal rate up to £50,000. This makes a pension fund a tax-efficient system. In Australia, I believe superannuation earnings are taxed at 15%, which is lower than the average marginal tax rate of approximately 31.5%. So, in essence, you would be around 16.5% better off by transferring more pre-taxed earnings into your pension/superannuation accounts. I believe access can be gained for UK pension funds once you are over 55 years old, so you could always look to direct more income into your pension fund and then withdraw this money afterwards to avoid paying the full income tax.

If you are young and a long way off retirement, it is still worth considering the differing investment options available. You could look at riskier investments for your funds, which could give you a better return in the long run. Age is critical in choosing the right investments because there will be fewer years to recover any lost ground with an investment when you are older. (It might be worth finding out about those who lost money in their funds during the global financial crisis of 2008.) I suggest you seek advice from a financial expert to work out the best options available that fit your own circumstances.

> **THE MONEY YOU PUT AWAY FOR YOUR PENSION FUND WILL QUALIFY FOR TAX RELIEF IF YOU INCREASE YOUR PENSION PAYMENTS**

QUICK LESSON 9: International money transfer accounts

If you are considering relocating and working/living abroad, you should look at opening an international money transfer account. This is to make sure you can take advantage of the best available exchange rate at that time when transferring money between your separate international accounts.

When I moved to the United Kingdom from Australia, my money was obviously in my Australian account. Initially, I found it difficult to open a British bank account because I couldn't provide proof of address from a utility bill as I had only just moved over! However, when I did open an account, I transferred around $5,000 Australian dollars direct from my Australian bank account. I can't remember exactly how much this converted to via this transfer, but let's say that the conversion rate for $1 Australian dollar was £0.55 British pounds, so I received approximately £2,750 sterling, which was not a great exchange rate at the time. At a later date I worked out that if I had transferred $5,000 via an international money transfer account (such as TransferWise), I would have received a higher rate of around £0.63 British pounds for every $1 Australian dollar. So, for this example, if I had initially used an international money transfer account, I would have received approximately an additional £400!

Always shop around online for the best deals and conversion rates when looking to set up an international money transfer account. For each transfer you will usually be charged a small fee. However, the exchange rate/conversion rate you receive is generally much better than from a bank-to-bank exchange between countries.

ENSURE YOU GET THE BEST AVAILABLE EXCHANGE RATE WHEN TRANSFERRING MONEY BETWEEN SEPARATE INTERNATIONAL ACCOUNTS

QUICK LESSONS FOR THE BUSINESS WORLD

The business world is a large part of the real world after we have finished our education. There are key skills required to be successful in this world, which I believe were barely discussed or taught in all my educational studies. Hopefully, you will gain a basic understanding of the quick lessons under this topic to then develop further in your current working life or in the future.

QUICK LESSON 10: The basics of how business works in the world we live in

Businesses generally operate to make a profit on their goods/services that are provided. You may have heard the saying 'money makes the world go round'. It is profit that makes a business healthy (as well as cash flow as discussed in Quick Lesson 18) and to grow in size. There are of course not-for-profit organisations, which generally raise money for a charity or service such as wildlife/conversation campaigns or medical research.

Profit is the difference between the sales from customers (revenue) and the costs (expenses) that are involved to operate the business. This simple fact is very important to understand as most companies all over the world follow this basic concept.

Profit = Revenue - Expenses

The business will be operating at a profit if the revenue generated is greater than the expenses. If the expenses are greater than the revenue, the business will be operating at a loss (or not operating at all for much longer). Profit is the money left over after all the bills have been paid. For example, if goods/services are sold for £200 and the costs associated to provide these goods/services are £150, the profit will be £50 or 25% of revenue (final profit/revenue).

The example below shows a specific business (you guessed it, a project management consultancy) and how this business makes a profit.

Let's assume the project management costs to a client/customer are £500 per day and is the total revenue. The costs/expenses are shown here:

Project manager salary £175 per day
Car allowances £15 per day
Other office staff salaries £10 per day
Office rent and bills £10 per day
Office IT £10 per day
Stationery £5 per day
Office expenses – tea, coffee, milk, etc. £5 per day

Total expenses = £175 + £15 + £10 + £10 + £10 + £5 + £5 = £230

Profit = revenue £500 – costs/expenses £230

Profit = £270 or 54% of revenue

Even if you are not responsible for managing and calculating the final profit of a business, it is good to know how profitable the business is and how profitable you are as an individual to the business, as this could be used as a negotiating tool for a pay rise. The project manager mentioned above may want to look at negotiating a salary increase due to his/her profitability!

PROFIT IS THE DIFFERENCE BETWEEN THE SALES FROM CUSTOMERS (REVENUE) AND THE COSTS (EXPENSES) THAT ARE INVOLVED TO OPERATE THE BUSINESS

QUICK LESSON 11: The benefits of networking

When I resigned from my job in Australia and set off to live in the United Kingdom, I wasn't worried or concerned about finding a new job in the same field. This was because I was networking with various companies before I left, which resulted in a few possible job options and prospects before I arrived. I then accepted a job offer just two days after I moved to Manchester. My referral to the company I work for currently came from a very simple lead and it happened because I played sport. I contacted a local lacrosse club that I wanted to join once I arrived in the city. They asked what I would be doing in Manchester; I said I was looking for work in construction project management. I was referred to one of the players at the club who worked in this field. He then sent out my CV to various suitable organisations, which resulted in them contacting me directly. The benefits of networking can be as simple as that.

I come from the city of Adelaide in Australia, which like all Australian cities is quite isolated from the rest of the world. The construction industry is largely built and run on reputation and good working relationships to survive (assuming pricing is similar throughout the industry). At the company I worked for, we all had pride in building relationships with everyone we worked with. This worked to our benefit because we were successful in obtaining repeat work from clients. This reputation also spread around the construction industry network to assist in gaining even more new clients. Our personable approach and networking attitude resulted in business success.

The saying 'it's not what you know, but who you know' can be very true in many aspects of life. To me, you gain good relationships with various people who may be willing to help if you are always personable with others (refer to Quick Lesson 52). You never know when one of your contacts or someone who is part of your network could come in handy. If your car was to break down, and you don't want to be ripped off by someone untrustworthy, do you have a contact who is a mechanic? If you are struggling to get a loan from a bank or a mortgage and require some help, do you know a mortgage broker who could help you? If possible, always be amiable with people and your network will expand, which will reap benefits in the real world.

> **THE SAYING 'IT'S NOT WHAT YOU KNOW, BUT WHO YOU KNOW' CAN BE VERY TRUE IN MANY ASPECTS OF LIFE**

QUICK LESSON 12: The importance of a curriculum vitae

A good quality CV is very important in the real world as it is your first step towards gaining employment. A CV is the first impression you make on your possible employer, which is vital to boost your chances of then getting a face-to-face interview. I am a strong believer that a lot of the time an employer has decided whether you are hireable from reading your application letter and CV, so you should spend time working on the content and presentation. Your CV is the best way of selling yourself in the first instance and enables you to highlight your skills and expertise. The potential employer can then determine how you will add value to the organisation you are applying to work for.

My advice for writing a good quality CV is ensuring that it is concisely written and accurate. Generally, I would keep it to no more than two pages and only include information that is actually relevant to the application. I applied for both project management and quantity surveying jobs when I was moving to the UK, as this is where I had experience and expertise. I produced two different CVs to highlight my relevant experience for both job types to increase my chances of gaining employment.

I recommend searching the internet for examples of good quality CVs as a guide. Below is a basic list of items an employer could be looking for on your CV.

- Personal details including address, email address, contact phone number, nationality and gender.

- Key personal skills you believe you have. You could ask a former employer, lecturer, teacher, or friend for opinions on your key skills if you are not sure.

- Your education and qualifications listed in chronological order, but I would only include those that are relevant to your application. For example, I would only list my university and post-high school qualifications when applying for a project management job.

- Employment history, but it may be best to only include employment history if you have previous experience in the same field, otherwise use other employment experience.

- For details of references, simply state that they can be provided upon request and ensure that your references are ready to be contacted.

I AM STRONG BELIEVER THAT A LOT OF THE TIME AN EMPLOYER HAS DECIDED WHETHER YOU ARE HIREABLE FROM READING YOUR APPLICATION LETTER AND CV

QUICK LESSON 13: Interviewing

With a good quality CV in place, the next important step to land that job you are after is by being able to interview well. Generally, the CV and its content will ensure you're offered an interview, which puts you in a good position to secure the job. However, how you perform and communicate in the interview and subsequent interviews can determine whether you receive a job offer or not.

Make sure you are well prepared for your interview. Carry out research on the internet about the organisation and make sure you believe that the company would be a good fit for you and your future if you were offered the job. In the interview, try to show an interest in what the organisation is about. For example, in the interview for the job I now have, I showed interest in the projects the company was currently working on, which I found via the company website. Research the company's standing within the industry they are involved in and who their market competitors might be. You could be asked what the company's competitive advantage is in the market and how you could add value to the business – so be prepared.

Search online for common interview questions and prepare your answers. You could rehearse a mock interview with a friend or family member to help you practice so you're not so nervous when it comes to the real thing!

Be prepared to sell yourself and your valuable skills in addition to the information on your CV. Try not to sound arrogant, but remember that you must try to promote yourself as no one else is going to do this for you. Prepare key positive attributes to discuss that you have displayed throughout your life which could also be backed up by your referees when they are contacted for a reference.

Remember, first impressions go a long way, so make sure you are dressed to impress and suitable for the role. Generally, in the professional world, you cannot go wrong with a black suit, white button-up long-sleeve shirt with a tie and black leather shoes for men and a conservative two piece shirt with a jacket, knee length skirt and dark shows for women. However, this will depend on the type of role you are applying for.

> **TRY NOT TO SOUND ARROGANT, BUT REMEMBER THAT YOU MUST TRY TO PROMOTE YOURSELF AS NO ONE ELSE IS GOING TO DO THIS FOR YOU**

QUICK LESSON 14: How to find a job

Now that you have a good CV and know some of the basics on how to interview well, it is time to find a job. This advice may sound unusual, but be careful contacting recruitment agencies to help you find a job. The reason I say this is because recruitment agencies charge a fee to any company that offers you a job they have referred you to. This means you are costing the new company before you have even completed a day's work there, which is not good for business! Because of the costs of recruitment agencies, many companies prefer potential employees to contact them directly with a covering letter and CV to avoid recruitment agencies altogether.

You should find as many companies that fit the type of place where you would like to work and contact them directly. Use the networks you have already created (refer to Quick Lesson 11) and issue your CV to as many companies as possible. Make sure you follow up with these companies via a phone call after you have sent/dropped off your CV because this will show a proactive approach.

If you are looking for full-time work, I believe you should make it a full-time occupation to try to find a job. If the role you are after has working hours of 8:00 a.m. to 5:30 p.m., then you should be working those hours to try to land a job. You could even dress up each day you are searching and keep your days free so you are ready and available should an interview opportunity arise.

The good news is because you have read Quick Lesson 11 and have been networking, you have already created contacts in the industry you want to work in. So get in touch as you might be surprised at what leads may come from these connections.

IF YOU ARE LOOKING FOR A FULL-TIME WORK, I BELIEVE YOU SHOULD MAKE IT A FULL-TIME OCCUPATION TO TRY TO FIND A JOB

QUICK LESSON 15: Get a job you can enjoy some days and tolerate on other days

There is a well-known saying 'choose a job you love, and you will never have to work a day in your life'. It is true that a small percentage of the population have a job that they love. This is, of course, a very low percentage. I believe it is unfair to tell people that they should love their job when very few people do. My advice is to find a job that you have an interest in or mostly enjoy and that you can tolerate for the rest of the time.

As a working professional, you will not carry out tasks that you really enjoy all the time because there will be others which may not be as enjoyable but are part of your role. If you can tolerate these more mundane/not as fun tasks, there is no real need to look elsewhere or change professions. For example, as a building contractor project manager, I really enjoyed delivering completed projects to our clients on time and under cost; however, I did not enjoy asking the subcontractors to rectify any snagging/defect issues at the end of a project. But this was required as part of my role and for the successful completion, so I could tolerate this part of the work and enjoy the other aspects.

Never be complacent in what you do for work, as there will always be other avenues and opportunities worth exploring to develop your career. You should never settle for a job just because you are comfortable in the role. Keep in mind that you have a job you enjoy most of the time, so it is not necessarily worth throwing away just because you don't love your job.

MY ADVICE IS TO FIND A JOB THAT YOU HAVE AN INTEREST IN OR MOSTLY ENJOY AND THAT YOU CAN TOLERATE FOR THE REST OF THE TIME

QUICK LESSON 16: The importance of being a team player

In everyday life, whether it is at a workplace or playing sport, we are generally part of a team that is required to work together and collaboratively to achieve a desired result. Your individual success can largely depend on others and how they perform as part of the team. So why not work together with these people to achieve the results you require?

My first piece of advice for being a good team player is to be a good listener. Listening can be one of the most important aspects of being a good team member because it can help you to understand your team members and how they operate. By listening and then collaborating, you can determine the team's goals and what your individual responsibilities are within the team. Never be afraid to express your own opinion in a personable manner, but always make sure you are respectful and listen to the other members of the team.

Make sure you show commitment and be a reliable part of the team. Always make sure that you undertake your fair share of work and are committed to achieving the results within your team. Strong team players care about their work and the work of the team they are involved in, and they show up to every meeting or training session they need to and on time. A reliable and committed team member will help with a positive culture within the group. These attributes will rub off on to other team members as well. The culture of a team will be a large determinant of the group's success.

Finally, always be respectful and supportive of your team members even if they are not doing the same. Good team players treat their fellow team members how they would like to be treated and they also support others to help get the job done. If one of your fellow team members is struggling, offer some assistance if you can because everyone can benefit from this.

THE CULTURE OF A TEAM WILL BE A LARGE DETERMINANT OF THE GROUP'S SUCCESS

QUICK LESSON 17: Customer-focused businesses are much more likely to succeed

If you ever decide to start your own business, no matter what industry or sector your business is in, remember that it must have customer focus at the core of its values if your business is to be sustainable and successful. This mindset should also be adopted for any business that you work for in the future. Some short-term business success might occur without having a strong customer focus; however, this will probably not last in the long term.

The construction industry is a prime example of this from my experience. I worked for a building contractor in South Australia that has a very strong customer focus, as well as a large focus on building relationships with everyone who they worked with. While I was working there between 2007 and 2014, the general commercial building sector in South Australia was quite stagnant with low economic growth. However, the company I worked for had high growth throughout most of these years mainly because of repeat business with well looked after customers as well as maintaining a good reputation within the industry. On the flip side, while working in the UK I have worked as a client-side project manager overseeing work by various building contractors, some of which have very poor customer focus and have not maintained good relationships with many other companies they are working with throughout the project. This could result in the client removing this contractor off their tender list. Also, most consultants working on the project won't recommend this contractor for any future projects

...cause of their non-relationship building approach to ... work.

Customers and clients are not necessarily the direct purchaser of your goods and services. Customers can be anyone involved in your work that could affect you getting future sales. In the construction industry, this may involve any company within your project team who could recommend or not recommend your business for future work, including project managers, development managers, architects, engineers, specialist consultants, subcontractors and suppliers, etc. If you maintain a personable approach, as mentioned in Quick Lesson 52, with all work colleagues, then this could go a long way to ensuring strong, sustainable business success.

SOME SHORT-TERM BUSINESS SUCCESS MIGHT OCCUR WITHOUT HAVING A STRONG CUSTOMER FOCUS; HOWEVER, THIS WILL PROBABLY NOT LAST IN THE LONG TERM

QUICK LESSON 18: What is cash flow and why is it important?

Cash flow is the total money transferred in and out of business accounts. I did not learn about the importance this until I started my first job as a project manager assistant, which is unusual because all businesses, large and small, generally rely on cash flow to survive and operate. You can have a profitable business but fail because you cannot manage cash flow effectively. Or, vice versa, you can have a low-profiting business but be successful because your business cash flow management is very good. Cash flow is also an asset for potential investors and lenders/creditors as well as helping to pay off any debt and having the funds available to expand a business.

The downside of having good cash flow in your own business may mean that this is at the expense of another organisation. However, this does not have to be the case if all suppliers and businesses work together to meet everyone's cash flow requirements in what we can call a 'win/win scenario'.

In basic terms, if possible and if it creates a win/win scenario for each party to have good cash flow management, you must ensure that your company receives payments for goods and/or services provided before you pay for the goods and/or services received (or at least over a similar time frame). The importance of cash flow really can depend on the size of the business and how much money is held within that business at one time. As previously mentioned, I work in the building industry. When working for a principal contractor, it was also very important for the company that payments were received from our clients before payments were issued to subcontractors/suppliers.

> **YOU CAN HAVE A PROFITABLE BUSINESS BUT FAIL BECAUSE YOU CANNOT MANAGE CASH FLOW EFFECTIVELY. OR, VICE VERSA, YOU CAN HAVE A LOW-PROFITING BUSINESS BUT BE SUCCESSFUL BECAUSE YOUR BUSINESS CASH FLOW MANAGEMENT IS VERY GOOD**

QUICK LESSON 19: Always look after your supply chain

In business, your supply chain can be the lifeblood of how you operate. The success of your business can largely depend on how good your relationship is with your supply chain and how well you treat them. As per Quick Lesson 18, this lesson can be adopted for any business that works in any industry or sector. For example, McDonalds relies on their beef suppliers for burgers; KFC relies on their chicken suppliers; Tesco relies on all the suppliers of their products to keep their shelves stocked; building contractors rely on subcontractors; and subcontractors rely on their material suppliers.

One of the best ways to look after your supply chain is to make sure your suppliers are paid for the goods and services they have provided within the timeframes you have previously agreed. This may sound like a very basic rule, but you would be surprised how often this doesn't happen within companies both nationally and internationally.

In the building industry all over the world it is a common accordance that if a client has not paid a principal building contractor for a certain aspect of work, then the principal contractor will not pay the subcontractors and suppliers as a result. Although this works from a cash flow perspective for the principal contractor, it is not fair to then pass this cash flow burden on to the supply chain who are working under a separate contract or agreement. Obviously, these occurrences could have a detrimental effect on the working relationships between these parties. The principal contractor I worked for in

South Australia always made sure that the supply chain were paid in accordance with the required time frames or that an agreement was reached in a timely manner. This ensured that strong relationships were maintained with the supply chain, which generally resulted in these companies sometimes going over and above to provide their services.

THE SUCCESS OF YOUR BUSINESS CAN LARGELY DEPEND ON HOW GOOD YOUR RELATIONSHIP IS WITH YOUR SUPPLY CHAIN AND HOW WELL YOU TREAT THEM

QUICK LESSON 20: Always move with the times and develop with economic conditions

Technology continues to advance and update throughout the world on a regular basis. Businesses and human resources associated should continually look to improve business operations via the latest technology. This will ensure the services provided to customers are continually improving with these updates, as well as guaranteeing that the company operations are as efficient as they can be to stay competitive and relevant within the economic market.

Most people will work from 16-23 years old to around 70 years on average. If you think about it, a 65-year-old in the current workforce would not have used a computer or mobile phone when they received their first pay cheque all those years ago because they weren't invented and available to use. In the future, there will no doubt be even more changes in information technology as we know it currently. So we should all be continually learning to ensure we keep up with these changes and advancements. Many people do not like change and prefer the old/usual ways of doing something. As time goes by, it seems more difficult to change an old habit or learn a new skill, but most of us are capable of continually developing and learning.

As part of my current project management role, I am responsible for undertaking snagging/defect inspections for the projects I am involved in to ensure that a complete and good quality product is handed over to the client. Previously, I had always handwritten these lists and then typed them up in a Microsoft Excel spreadsheet after the inspections, which was a very time-consuming process. Now, I have a programme on my tablet where I can input the items from the site as I walk around. This technology has assisted me in completing the work in approximately half the time, so my productivity has increased for this particular part of my job and it frees up my time to complete other tasks.

> **AS TIME GOES BY, IT SEEMS MORE DIFFICULT TO CHANGE AN OLD HABIT OR LEARN A NEW SKILL, BUT MOST OF US ARE CAPABLE OF CONTINUALLY DEVELOPING AND LEARNING**

QUICK LESSON 21: Learn to take and accept negative feedback

One of the best pieces of advice I can give you that I have learnt in the real world is to always take feedback on board, especially if it is negative, and then learn from this feedback. One of the general aspects of Millennials when they enter the workforce is that they cannot seem to handle adverse feedback; they appear to take it personally and tend to quit their job as a result. Constructive feedback is the best way we can learn and develop to achieve our goals in various aspects of life. So, feedback – positive or constructive – should always be welcomed and taken on board. If, on the flip side, you are providing feedback for others, always do so in a personable and respectful manner to get the best results from people.

Remember that everyone receives feedback. Some people, including politicians and sports stars, receive instant feedback from a lot of people! The best sporting professionals will generally take any feedback received from the right people, such as a coach, and then learn from this to become a better player.

When I was working as a project administrator for a head building contractor in Australia after university, I was given a lot of responsibility from a fairly young age – and I thought I was a lot more experienced and knew a lot more than I actually did at the time. Generally, I was working in teams with industry professionals, such as architects, engineers and subcontractors, that had a lot more experience and expertise than I did. But I always seemed to think I knew best, which resulted in issues with these team members on a few projects. The consequence was that my boss at the time sat me down and gave me some honest and quite brutal feedback. I came out of this meeting feeling very annoyed and upset. Although, when I thought about it, a lot of the criticism was true. I had two options at the time: 1) quit my job, look elsewhere and possibly not learn from my mistakes. Or 2) take on board the feedback received and prove that I am capable of developing into the employee my company required. I chose option 2, which resulted in great career development; and I believe this is still the backbone for how I operate to this day.

FEEDBACK IS THE BEST WAY WE CAN LEARN AND DEVELOP TO ACHIEVE OUR GOALS IN VARIOUS ASPECTS OF LIFE. SO, FEEDBACK – POSITIVE OR CONSTRUCTIVE – SHOULD ALWAYS BE WELCOMED AND TAKEN ON BOARD

QUICK LESSON 22: How to negotiate

I do not believe that I was specifically taught how to negotiate effectively at school, but we use negotiation in lots of different ways in various aspects of everyday life. I believe the way we need to negotiate in varying situations depends on who and what we are negotiating with, and how many times we may or may not have to negotiate in the future. In life, there are one-off deals and then there are deals that could take place on an ongoing basis.

As an example, a one-off deal could be purchasing a car. For this type of negotiation, it is very unlikely you will be dealing with the car salesperson/private seller ever again. So, for this reason, I suggest you look for the best possible car at the lowest possible price, as you don't need to keep an ongoing relationship with the seller. If they don't like your offer, they can refuse to accept it because it's their prerogative. Just make sure you carry out this negotiation in an ethical and respectful way to the other party.

In my experience, I believe you should negotiate differently with people you would like an ongoing relationship with, or with those who could affect ongoing relationships or business in the future. Essentially, you don't want to negotiate or take advantage of a situation so you get what you want but the other person's needs/wants are completely neglected. As an example, I worked for a principal building contractor in Australia who were personable in how they negotiated with their clients by ensuring that they were not exposed to any unnecessary risks and that the client's needs and wants were also maintained. This negotiating strategy often resulted in good client satisfaction, repeat business, and positive referrals and recommendations to other clients throughout the industry. I have also worked on projects with other building contractors in the UK who took advantage of the strong negotiation position they held. This may have helped them to obtain what they wanted, but it was at the expense of the client's needs/wants. The result was an unsatisfied client, who may not give this contractor any future work or recommend them to other potential clients, and a poor reputation within the local industry.

There is a lot of information online where negotiating skills are taught in detail, so I suggest you research this topic further because these skills will help you in many aspects of life.

I BELIEVE THE WAY WE NEED TO NEGOTIATE IN VARYING SITUATIONS DEPENDS ON WHO AND WHAT WE ARE NEGOTIATING WITH AND HOW MANY TIMES WE MAY OR MAY NOT HAVE TO NEGOTIATE IN THE FUTURE

QUICK LESSON 23: The importance of productivity

The more productive you are in your job, the more valuable you will be as a member of staff. Also, generally, the productivity levels of any organisation and its employees reflect how successful, competitive and sustainable the business operations are. I say 'generally' because it can really depend on the type of work you are carrying out. For example, if you work at McDonalds as a burger maker, you will be more productive if you can put together a fresh burger and clean up after yourself quickly. However, if you are a business development manager, one of the only real ways your productivity might be measured is by how many new clients you bring into a business. A position such as a business development manager is more of a relationship-building role. Whereas, a worker at a fast-food outlet is required to perform a high level of work output.

Completing a high level of work output within certain job roles does not necessarily result in being productive or having good productivity. This is because completing work that is not required or is not a top priority may not add to the productivity of a business. Also, if your time management is not great (refer to Quick Lesson 54) and you do not work efficiently, then this may also affect your individual productivity.

To be productive, you must work out your role within the business and make sure you are working to your own set budget or improve on the productivity that you have been budgeted against. For example, when I was working as a project manager for a principal contractor, I would have set target budgets for each year that were based on the target profit margins for the projects I was managing. Let's say that one year my target budget was $800,000 and in that year I reached $1,000,000, then you could say in basic terms that I had increased productivity against my projected target budget. At the same time, however, I had to ensure that I met other job role targets, such as building relationships with customers and suppliers. I could have easily reached the productivity levels for the year, but I could not do this at the expense of the customers or suppliers as it would not have been viable. This is a very important point when looking at productivity because it should not be at the expense of sustainable business operations.

Never be afraid to discuss your productivity levels with your colleagues and managers to ensure you receive constructive feedback. This will ensure you are continually improving your own productivity and the levels set within the team or organisation.

THE PRODUCTIVITY LEVELS OF ANY ORGANISATION AND ITS EMPLOYEES REFLECT HOW SUCCESSFUL, COMPETITIVE AND SUSTAINABLE THE BUSINESS OPERATIONS ARE

QUICK LESSON 24: How to write an effective email

Writing effective emails is a valuable skill for the real world. I believe in the current workplace I am involved in, emails tend to be overused and communication via phone calls or face-to-face tend to be underused simply because it is usually easier for someone to send an email than talk to the person or pick up the phone. Emails can be a great way to communicate a point of view without having any kind of emotion or body language involved, and emails are also a great way to document a conversation that has taken place. With this in mind, emotion should be avoided at all costs because an email can easily be miscommunicated by another party especially because there is no body language, facial expressions or tone of voice that can be picked up by the other person.

The best lesson I have learnt when sending important emails in the workplace is to make sure you put yourself in the shoes of the receiver. I always draft important emails first, then walk away from the computer, grab a coffee and come back to reread it as if I were the recipient. When reviewing it, make sure you ask yourself how you feel reading the email. Does it get the message across in an informative and respectful manner? Is there any emotion that could be miscommunicated by the receiving party? Are there grammar or spelling errors within the email? From this review, make sure you are satisfied with the content and send the email if appropriate. Make sure that you understand the emotional feeling you receive from reviewing the email. If there is too much emotion involved, rewrite or edit the email before sending.

If possible, only use emails to issue/distribute documents and to record an event for discussion that could be used for reference at a later date. Trying to problem solve or resolve complex issues over emails can be completely counterproductive, so this should be carried out face-to-face as much as practically possible.

> **THE BEST LESSON I HAVE LEARNT WHEN SENDING IMPORTANT EMAILS IN THE WORKPLACE IS TO MAKE SURE YOU PUT YOURSELF IN THE SHOES OF THE RECEIVER**

QUICK LESSON 25: How to see the big picture

As per Quick Lesson 17, customer-focused businesses are much more likely to succeed. One of the ways of being a very customer-focused business or employee is to understand the bigger picture. In my opinion, the bigger picture is working towards sustainable business success via repeat business or customer referrals for new clients. Aim for sustainable success in what you do instead of looking to make a quick dollar/pound at the expense of someone else as that could affect the bigger picture.

I will use the example of the principal contractor that I worked for in Adelaide as a business that really could, and I believe still does, see the bigger picture and always works with the view of having sustainable long-term success rather than unsustainable short-term success. When I was an employee there, we always put the customer first and the relationship with the customer was held in very high regard, even if we thought we were right and they were wrong. We would lose money on certain deals/negotiations knowing that we could get repeat business and have a good reputation within the local industry if the client/customer was satisfied. As a result of this business understanding, their bigger picture is that they have now grown to almost double in size and doubled their revenue over the last three to four years.

On the other hand, I have worked with another principal contractor who did not seem to see or understand the bigger picture. They received work from a client I work for as a result of acquiring another contractor. This contractor did not work with a customer-first approach, so on numerous occasions they negotiated in a way that always put themselves and the profit ahead of the needs and requirements of the client/customer. This is especially true for their project specific manager who continually works in a way that puts their short-term business needs ahead of the customer, which in my opinion is not sustainable. Now, I cannot predict the future, but I am sure this contractor will not gain any work with our client as a result and they may have difficulty securing future work within the region because of their reputation from this specific project.

Does the company you work for see the bigger picture? Do you see the bigger picture? Think about how you can individually work towards sustainable success in business.

THE BIGGER PICTURE IS WORKING TOWARDS SUSTAINABLE SUCCESS VIA REPEAT BUSINESS OR CUSTOMER REFERRALS FOR NEW CLIENTS

QUICK LESSON 26: Meeting efficiency

Taking part and running meetings is a large part of many people's professional lives in the real world. An important skill to have is the ability to make meetings run smoothly and efficiently. I've been involved in many meetings (specifically in the United Kingdom) that run a lot longer than they need to and with no real productivity. The more effectively meetings are run in any industry will result in increased efficiency and productivity as a whole, which is obviously better for business. Some of the meetings I am involved in might have upwards of 20 people and can last for 4-5 hours, which is a lot of money for that meeting if it isn't efficient and doesn't achieve what is required.

My advice for managing/participating in meetings:

1. Always show up on time and hopefully this motivates other people to do the same. By getting to meetings on time, you are showing your work colleagues that their time is important to you and vice versa. Attendees cause a distraction when they turn up late, which does not help the meeting to run efficiently.

2. Have an agenda in place and stick to the itinerary as best as possible. Issue the agenda to all the attendees so they are aware of the discussion points and can prepare for the meeting.

3. Do not discuss a specific agenda item more than necessary. There can be items or action points that can't always be resolved at the time, so ensure discussions don't overrun and try to move on to the next item with an action plan in place to deal with any outstanding issues.

4. Make people accountable by agreeing dates and timings when certain actions are to be completed, and then review the action items from the previous meetings to hold people to account.

5. Have an agreed and achievable time frame for a meeting. For example, if it should take two hours, try to stick to this time frame as efficiently as possible.

6. Ensure that the meeting minutes are concise and to the point so they are easy to follow after the meeting has ended. Also, aim to issue the minutes within 48 hours, as this will help to make sure that everyone is clear of any actions required in an efficient manner.

AN IMPORTANT SKILL TO HAVE IS THE ABILITY TO MAKE MEETINGS RUN SMOOTHLY AND EFFICIENTLY

QUICK LESSON 27: How to problem solve in the workplace

In high school, we generally learn by being told information, reading about a subject or by asking questions on a topic. Unfortunately, this way of learning does not necessarily equip us with the skill of problem solving in difficult and stressful situations in the real world.

When I was working as assistant project manager early in my career, I learnt some very valuable lessons on problem solving. When I had an issue or a question in relation to a problem that I didn't know the answer to, I always used to pester my boss and continually ask him questions. This was obviously very disruptive to my boss at the time and it didn't teach me how to solve the problem on my own. After a while, my boss told me to go away and not come back to him with any questions until I had worked through the problem and come up with a possible resolution myself. Once I had done this, I could go back to him with the proposed solution. He would then advise whether this was right or wrong in his opinion. If the solution was wrong, he would explain why. I could learn from this for the next time that type of issue or scenario came up.

I believe we learn how to problem solve by working it out ourselves and coming up with a solution whether it is right or wrong. If our solution is wrong, then that's OK as we can learn from this. A lot of the time we learn more from our mistakes than from doing something correctly. You, of course, will then need to make sure that you don't make the same mistake twice! Take the initiative now and start solving problems. This is a highly valuable skill for the real world and especially in the business world.

> **A LOT OF THE TIME WE LEARN MORE FROM OUR MISTAKES THAN FROM DOING SOMETHING CORRECTLY**

QUICK LESSONS ON PROPERTY AND REAL ESTATE

QUICK LESSON 28: Saving for a house deposit

There has been a lot of discussion lately in both Australia and the United Kingdom about housing affordability and the difficulties the Millennial generation face in being able to own their own home. There are cities within these countries that have high median house prices, such as London and Sydney, but there are also other cities and areas with very affordable houses. My advice is to get on the property ladder as early as possible because the first property purchase is generally the hardest. Then you can always look to upgrade and move up the property ladder in areas where you would like to live. If you live in Sydney, have you ever thought about relocating to a city with more affordable housing such as Adelaide? If you live in London, have you ever thought about relocating to a city with more affordable housing such as Manchester?

I believe one of the biggest challenges people face in being able to buy a property is having a cash deposit/savings in place. My advice is to work out the approximate value of the property you can get a mortgage on and would like to buy. For example, the current median house price in Adelaide is approximately $452,000. To purchase a property of this value (depending on the bank and loan conditions) you would need a deposit of around $45,200, along with money for fees and stamp duty at around $23,000. So the total would be approximately $68,200. With this total in mind, you can work out how much you need to save each week to start purchasing a property. As an example, if you can save $500 each per week as a couple ($1,000 per couple per week), you would be in a position to purchase a property valued at $452,000 in Adelaide within approximately 70 weeks (if you have no savings at all to start with!).

As suggested in Quick Lesson 3, a good way to save money is by recording your expenditure so you can analyse where all your money is going on a daily and weekly basis. You might have to make life decisions to work out what you can actually spend and still be able to save enough to purchase a property.

Alternatively, my advice to parents (if you can afford it) is if you have equity in your own house or properties that you own, you could release some of this to contribute to your child's house deposit and think of it as a good investment for the future. If you do give them the money, just make sure it is actually spent on a house deposit and nothing else!

AS AN EXAMPLE, IF YOU CAN SAVE $500 EACH PER WEEK AS A COUPLE ($1,000 PER COUPLE PER WEEK), YOU WOULD BE IN A POSITION TO PURCHASE A PROPERTY VALUED AT $452,000 IN ADELAIDE WITHIN APPROXIMATELY 70 WEEKS (IF YOU HAVE NO SAVINGS AT ALL TO START WITH!)

QUICK LESSON 29: What is property equity and why is it important?

Once again, this is another lesson I was not familiar with until I was in my twenties. Property equity is the difference between the property's market value and the amount originally paid (minus deposit/stamp duty, etc.) or the current mortgage debt. For example, if your home is worth £300,000 and your mortgage is £225,000, the equity on your property is £75,000. The value of the property may have increased since the purchase for various reasons; however, the most common are due to renovations/improvements carried out and general housing inflation (increase in value) in the area.

The reason I believe this is important is that once you have equity in your home/property, you can release this money by remortgaging the property (refer to Quick Lesson 31 for more information). This equity can then purchase another property, which can be used as an investment. This process can be repeated numerous times to simply purchase various properties just by using the equity obtained from others.

The downside of being able to obtain equity as cash is that it's easy to use the money to go on holidays and purchase luxury goods such as cars, boats, etc. This is not recommended because you will be worse off financially. Items such as cars do not increase in value, so you will not see a return on the equity. However, if you purchase another property with the equity obtained, then the new property should (for various reasons depending on where/when you buy as growth is not guaranteed) start increasing in value and provide further equity.

PROPERTY EQUITY IS THE DIFFERENCE BETWEEN THE PROPERTY'S MARKET VALUE AND THE AMOUNT ORIGINALLY PAID (MINUS DEPOSIT/STAMP DUTY, ETC.) OR THE CURRENT MORTGAGE DEBT. FOR EXAMPLE, IF YOUR HOME IS WORTH £300,000 AND YOUR MORTGAGE IS £225,000, THE EQUITY ON YOUR HOME/PROPERTY IS £75,000

QUICK LESSON 30: Ways to add value to your property

There are quite a few ways to increase the value of your property and gain equity as mentioned in Quick Lesson 29. Generally, my advice is to add as much liveable space at the lowest possible price (just in case you weren't aware that the lower the price the better!). You can do the maths on what type of value your extension/renovation works could add to your property. For example, if four-bedroom houses with additional lounge rooms within your area are selling for around £300,000, then you can calculate how much equity you could gain on your property by completing a similar extension/renovation. If your three-bedroom semi-detached property is worth £250,000 (you know this as you have had a RICS (Royal Institute for Chartered Surveyors) valuation survey completed) and the cost to upgrade to a four-bedroom property with an additional lounge is about £25,000, you should be able to gain an additional £25,000 of equity (before tax) after deducting the costs to carry out the work.

I've heard that loft conversions in the United Kingdom can add the most amount of value as a percentage of the cost. This is probably because it creates more liveable space, such as an additional bedroom, without having to complete major structural building work (usually just roof frame amendments are required as well as adding a staircase).

My list of possible ways to add value to your property:

1. Loft conversion – As above, convert your loft space into additional liveable space, which could be an additional bedroom, games room or office space.

2. Garage conversion – You could convert a garage area into a liveable space, i.e. additional lounge/study/bedroom, which is similar to the loft conversion.

3. Convert front garden – Increase parking in this area as off-road parking will always add value. Also, if you have converted your garage into a liveable space, it would be a good idea to provide a good amount of parking space.

4. Conservatory extension – This will create additional liveable space and they are usually less expensive than a brick wall extension.

5. Neutral colours – Use non-controversial colours when renovating as this should make the property easier to sell.

When completing your house renovations, look to employ the professionals who will interrupt your life balance as little as possible. Also, obtain three different quotes and seek references from previous clients.

> **GENERALLY, MY ADVICE IS TO ADD AS MUCH LIVEABLE SPACE TO THE PROPERTY AT THE LOWEST POSSIBLE PRICE**

QUICK LESSON 31: What is remortgaging and what are the benefits?

I really wish I knew about remortgaging and the benefits when I finished my education and entered the property market. Remortgaging is basically entering into an alternative mortgage loan with another bank lender when you already have a mortgage on a property.

I believe there are two real benefits when remortgaging a property. The first is to get a better deal from an alternative lender. Let's say you are on a variable interest loan with Bank A and they are offering a rate of 4.50%. Then an alternative bank, which we will call Bank B, are offering a variable rate of 4.20%, you can of course jump ship and change to get a better deal on your loan. If you are on a fixed-interest mortgage, you could also change lenders to get a better deal for your fixed rate.

The second benefit when you remortgage a property is that it will be revalued against the property's current worth compared to the original purchase price. The difference is called equity, as discussed earlier, which is the excess cash that can be obtained to then possibly buy another property or carry out house renovations. Now, be warned, as mentioned in Quick Lesson 29, it is not recommended that you use the equity from your remortgage/refinancing to spend on items that will not give you a good investment or monetary return on your purchase, such as buying a car or going on holiday. However, you can use the equity from a property in any way you like; just beware that now there will be more money to pay off on your loan than you owed previously.

> **EQUITY IS THE DIFFERENCE BETWEEN WHAT THE PROPERTY IS NOW WORTH COMPARED TO THE PURCHASE PRICE**

QUICK LESSON 32: What is rental yield and why is it important?

Rental yield is the annual rental income you receive from a property as a percentage of the property value. Calculations on this basis can be used to determine the best available properties to generate a good monthly monetary return. As mentioned later in Quick Lesson 53, owning rental properties that generate revenue every month is a good way to have an extra income stream without taking up a lot of time outside your main job.

Different parts of the world and different areas of countries will generate differing rental yields, so you should research the property markets to determine where you would like to invest. I believe the easiest way is to look at property websites such as www.rightmove.co.uk in the UK and www.realestate.com.au in Australia to see properties for sale and rent in various areas. For example, if you find a two-bedroom terrace that is listed for sale at £80,000 and there are similar terraced houses in the same area with a rental of £600 per month, then the rental yield will be £600 x 12 / £80,000 = 9%, which is very a good yield. If you bought this property for £80,000 with an interest-only loan (interest rate say 4%) and a deposit of 25%, then the repayments would be approximately £200 per month. The income from this property would be approximately £400 (minus any monthly costs such as maintenance, property management fees, insurance, tax, etc.), which is a very handy extra income stream that may take up very little of your time.

CALCULATIONS ON THIS BASIS CAN BE USED TO DETERMINE THE BEST AVAILABLE PROPERTIES TO GENERATE A GOOD MONTHLY MONETARY RETURN

QUICK LESSON 33: Buy property from motivated sellers

When looking to buy investment properties, it is financially beneficial to purchase properties below the market value. This will ensure that there is already equity in the property once you have completed the purchase. The equity can then be used to fund deposits for further property investments or renovation work to add value to your portfolio, as explained in Quick Lesson 29.

As an example, if you were to purchase a property for £95,000 and then a valuation report valued the property at £110,000, you could claim £15,000 as equity by remortgaging the property. Also, by purchasing properties below the market value, you will be able to ride out any downturns in the market that may occur over time.

If you're wondering how this can be done, it is by purchasing properties from motivated sellers. Motivated sellers are generally after a quick sale rather than waiting for the best price offer. There are many reasons why a seller could be willing to accept a sale price below the value of the property, so your job is to work out why and provide a solution to their problem. If the reason is because they require a quick sale to pay off a debt, for example, then you should make sure you can provide a quick sale to solve this problem. To enable this, make sure you have approved finance or cash available, a cash deposit, solicitors who can work quickly, as well as possibly offering the seller a good solicitor to complete a quick sale, and ensure that you are not involved in a chain where you have to sell your property to finance the new property.

Some possible reasons why the seller could be a motivated seller:

- The former owner has deceased
- The owners have separated or divorced
- Emigrating overseas
- Issues with chains
- Cash flow problems

MOTIVATED SELLERS ARE GENERALLY AFTER A QUICK SALE RATHER THAN WAITING FOR THE BEST PRICE OFFER

QUICK LESSONS ON GOVERNMENTS AND THE ECONOMY

QUICK LESSON 34: Basics of how the government works

The government systems in the United Kingdom and Australia are very similar in how they operate because the Australian parliamentary system is generally based on the United Kingdom's Westminster-style government. The Prime Minister in both countries leads the government with support from the Cabinet and ministers. As part of this lesson, I will generally focus on the Australian federal government system. The Prime Minister becomes the leader of the government after firstly becoming leader of the party it is representing. Then after a general election, the political party that has the support of the majority of members of the House of Representatives becomes the governing party and the leader of this party becomes the Prime Minister of the nation.

In Australia, there is the Federal Government, which includes the federation of six states as well as two self-governing states. There is also a state government for each of the six states that are run in a very similar way to the federal government but just at state level.

The constitution of Australia gives legislative power (the power to make laws) to the parliament. This parliament consists of the Queen, who is represented by the Governor-General, and the two houses, which are the House of Representatives and the Senate. The representatives of these houses are elected by the people of the nation who have enrolled to vote, which is a legal requirement in Australia (even if you are living overseas). The parliament passes through legislation (laws) that have to be agreed by both houses of parliament for the proposed legislation to become law.

Another main role of this parliament is to authorise the government of the Executive, which is agreeing how to spend public money (generally raised via taxation mentioned later in Quick Lesson 39), scrutinising the administrative actions undertaken by the government and serving as a forum of debate in relation to public policies.

This quick lesson provides a basic overview of how the government operates in Australia and the United Kingdom. There are various ways other governments operate in nations all over the world that can be researched further.

THE CONSTITUTION OF AUSTRALIA GIVES LEGISLATIVE POWER (THE POWER TO MAKE LAWS) TO THE PARLIAMENT

QUICK LESSON 35: What is globalisation?

Globalisation is a term that I do not remember hearing in my school years; however, this is very important in the world that we currently live in. Globalisation is how countries and continents are linked together around the world via business and trade. It is the process where businesses develop international influence or operate on an international scale.

Many countries rely on the economic success of others for their own success and well-being due to the quantum of goods and services that are traded around the world. If you are living in a developed country, have you noticed how many goods that you use and consume in your day-to-day life are made in China? China's economy relies to a certain extent on exporting goods to Western countries, such as the USA and the UK, and these countries rely on goods being used and consumed in their daily lives. If those trade routes were to end right now, many people could be out of work and the cost of living in Western countries could go up dramatically. This would result in an increase in inflation, which is a term you may have heard before.

There are varying opinions around the world as to the positives and negatives associated with globalisation and how it affects people's lives. For example, steel for the building industry can be produced at a much cheaper rate in China than in Australia. The main reason for this is due to varying salaries and labour rates that are paid in each country. Because China can produce this product cheaper, the Australian industry, for example, may have suffered as a result affecting the livelihoods of many people. This could be an example of the types of reasons why the Brexit vote came through and why Donald Trump was elected in the United States because both parties campaigned against the negative effects of globalisation.

Either way, I believe that globalisation is here to stay and I strongly believe that we should embrace the positives of globalisation across borders to all work together for a better world.

GLOBALISATION IS HOW COUNTRIES AND CONTINENTS ARE LINKED TOGETHER AROUND THE WORLD VIA BUSINESS AND TRADE

QUICK LESSON 36: Basics of left-wing and right-wing politics

I learnt very little in relation to politics at school and even less about the specific policies and beliefs of the major parties in the country where I grew up. You may have heard the terms 'left-wing politics' and 'right-wing politics', but what do they actually mean? See below for details on what the general population believe they would be getting by voting for the parties that generally fall under each category.

Right-wing politics:
I believe the policies of these parties are generally of a conservative or traditional nature. They tend to believe in economic growth and the survival of the fittest in a competitive environment. There are beliefs of economic freedom, that businesses should not be regulated and that everyone should do what is best for themselves to survive in the economy. Right-wing politics believe that there should be freedom to succeed. They are not specifically interested in equality or shared services to bridge the gap between the rich and the poor, such as the health and education services that can be provided. In the UK, the major parties that focus on right-wing policies are the Conservatives and UKIP, which both generally believed that Britain should leave the European Union (although former Prime Minister David Cameron campaigned to remain in the EU). In Australia, the major party that focuses on right-wing policies is the Liberal Party. In the United States, the Republicans are considered a right-wing party

Left-wing politics:

I believe the policies of these parties are generally of a progressive nature as they look towards the future and plan for sustainability. The left-wing political parties generally believe in equality and look at ways to support all people within the nation via support services. These parties believe in wealth distribution through taxation to support services such as the National Health Service (in the United Kingdom) and benefit payments for the unemployed and disabled. These political parties believe that big businesses should be regulated to support the interest of all the people, that climate change is an issue and that countrywide taxation funded action on the climate is necessary. In the UK and Australia, the major parties that focus on policies resulting in these types of beliefs are the Labour Party and the Green Party, which both generally believed that Britain should remain in the European Union. In the United States, the Democrats are considered a left-wing party.

Which beliefs do you feel most strongly about?

IN THE UK, THE MAJOR PARTIES THAT FOCUS ON RIGHT-WING POLICIES ARE THE CONSERVATIVES AND UKIP, WHICH BOTH GENERALLY BELIEVED THAT BRITAIN SHOULD LEAVE THE EUROPEAN UNION

QUICK LESSON 37: How to Vote

Now that you have a basic understanding of left-wing and right-wing politics from Quick Lesson 36, you should make sure that you are enrolled and able to vote at all upcoming elections in your area and nationally. In Australia, it is compulsory to vote if you are over 18 years old. In the United Kingdom, it is not compulsory to vote, but it is highly recommended. If you decide not to enrol to vote or vote in any specific election, remember that you should never complain about the politics within your country as you decided not to have your say in how your local area or country is run!

Firstly, you have to make sure that you are registered on the electoral roll, which is updated annually. In the United Kingdom, you can enrol to vote online or via the post if you are over 16 (you can only vote when you are 18 years or older) and if you are a British citizen. For more details, I suggest you research online for any specific requirements. The other benefit of being on the electoral roll, as mentioned in Quick Lesson 5, is that this should help your credit score and overall capacity to successfully apply for a loan from a lending organisation.

Once you have registered to vote, there are three ways you can vote in any given election:

1) In person at a polling station – The council should send you a polling card. This advises where you can vote in person at a polling station, which are usually located within public buildings such as schools or local halls and are generally open between 7 a.m. and 10 p.m. on election days. Once you are at these locations, you must enter the polling booth, follow the instructions on the polling card and place the card into the ballot box.

2) By post – You must apply for a postal vote if you are going to vote this way, which would generally be because you are away or overseas. I suggest finding out the exact requirements on the government/local council website.

3) By proxy (someone else voting on your behalf) – Once again, you would have to apply to vote by proxy and there are specific circumstances where this will be allowed, such as not being able to vote in person due to having a medical issue or disability.

THE OTHER BENEFIT OF BEING ON THE ELECTORAL ROLL, AS MENTIONED IN QUICK LESSON 5, IS THAT THIS SHOULD HELP YOUR CREDIT SCORE AND OVERALL CAPACITY TO SUCCESSFULLY APPLY FOR A LOAN FROM A LENDING ORGANISATION

QUICK LESSON 38: The rise of nationalism

While writing this book, Donald Trump won the US election and was sworn into the White House as President of the United States of America. In June 2016, the United Kingdom held a referendum in which the majority voted to leave the European Union. At the time, both victories were hugely against the odds and unexpected for most people in those countries and around the world. I feel compelled to write about this, as I do not think school curriculums will catch up in time to teach students about this movement commonly known as nationalism.

The people who voted in the US presidential election and EU referendum have their own personal views as to why they voted the way they did. Of course, this will vary in nature. However, my general view is that the results of these elections were mainly due to a nationalist mentality of over half of the people (or in Trump's case, the majority of states that he needed to win as Hilary Clinton won the overall majority vote). I believe this simplistic view is because Donald Trump's policies are what he believes will protect the people of America via closed borders and by bolstering internal manufacturing rather than boosting trade routes with other countries throughout the world. I believe the result of the EU referendum in simplistic terms was to stop open borders with European countries, as over half of the British population wanted to protect their country from people who are migrating from other areas within the European Union.

Why is this and why did it happen? I think this is because many people believe they have/had a better culture and way of life in their own countries and want to protect this for their own personal interests without considering the impact this would have in a globalised world community. This idea really worries me, as I believe over history generally whenever a race or group of people feel they are more superior to other groups of people it usually ends in warfare and conflict, which is not beneficial to anyone in this world or future generations.

I am a born and bred Australian who has lived in Australia, the United States of America and the United Kingdom. My heritage is relatively unknown, but I believe that I have ancestry from Australia, England, Germany, Denmark, Scotland, Ireland and the Netherlands, which is a similar story to many people around the world. I wouldn't be where I am today if my ancestors hadn't migrated to other countries, so I believe the way forward is through open minds and a supportive, functioning globalised world.

> **MANY PEOPLE BELIEVE THEY HAVE/HAD A BETTER CULTURE AND WAY OF LIFE IN THEIR OWN COUNTRIES AND WANT TO PROTECT THIS FOR THEIR OWN PERSONAL INTERESTS WITHOUT CONSIDERING THE IMPACT THIS WOULD HAVE IN A GLOBALISED WORLD COMMUNITY**

QUICK LESSON 39: Basics of how the tax system works

In school, I can't remember being taught about the tax system or how it works, which is unusual because most people pay tax on their earnings. As the saying goes, there are only two certainties in life: death and taxes. So, unless you're conducting illegal activities and not declaring your income fully or you're laundering money, you will have to pay tax.

Tax is a compulsory monetary contribution to the revenue of the government. Tax is generally levied on workers' incomes and business profits; however, it is also added to the cost of some goods and services. Most countries around the world have what is called a 'tiered tax system', which means there isn't a flat tax rate for what you must pay and the payment rate depends on your yearly income. For example, as of early 2018, in the United Kingdom you are in the basic rate bracket if you earn between £11,851 to £46,350, which has a rate of 20%. If you earn between £46,351 and £150,000, you will pay a rate of 40% tax as a higher rate taxpayer. The tax rate is 0% for anyone earning under £11,850.

The government uses the tax contributed to pay for various services in the economy such as those listed below.

- Education – schools and universities

- Health – hospitals, emergency services and the NHS (National Health Service) in the UK

- Pension funds

- Transportation – roads, bridges, buses, rail network, etc.

- Housing and environment – national parks and government supplied houses, etc.

- Interest and federal debt

- State pensions and social services

The government divides these sectors into three categories: mandatory spending, discretionary spending, and interest or federal debt.

UNLESS YOU'RE CONDUCTING ILLEGAL ACTIVITIES AND NOT DECLARING YOUR INCOME FULLY OR YOU'RE LAUNDERING MONEY, YOU WILL HAVE TO PAY TAX

QUICK LESSON 40: Completing a tax return

In Australia, everyone who earns a monetary income should complete and issue a tax return to the Australian Taxation Office (ATO). There are items you may have bought as part of your job that you can offset against your income, such as petrol, clothes, stationery and computers, etc. My advice is to keep all these receipts in a shoebox throughout the year (the tax year in the UK runs from 6th April to the following 5th April) for what could be described as work-related expenses. You may also receive a rebate from the tax office simply because your employer has deducted more tax from your pay in error or if you have been allocated the wrong tax code. Always make sure you complete a tax return for these reasons.

Remember the information about networking in Quick Lesson 11 because it is always good to have a contact who is an accountant specialising in tax returns. They will be able to show you the best way to complete this in order to maximise your return to the government or even possibly minimise your losses. You can complete an ATO tax return online at www.ato.gov.au or via a paper copy which is then posted. However, my advice is to complete the tax return with the help of an accountant who has the expertise. You can of course pay for an accountant to complete the tax return for you if you are short of time. If you use an accountant, make sure it is someone who can be trusted with your finances. Shop around and obtain at least three quotes so you find an accountant with the best rate and recommendations.

YOU MIGHT ACTUALLY GET A NICE SURPRISE WHEN YOU COMPLETE YOUR TAX RETURN AS YOU CAN GET SOME MONEY BACK FROM THE GOVERNMENT

QUICK LESSON 41: How international currency exchange rates are determined

Throughout your life, you will hear about exchange rates and how various currencies compare against each other as a result of economic influences. But what does this all mean and how are the currency exchange rates of nations determined?

An exchange rate is the rate at which one nation's currency is exchanged for another.

Currency is continually bought and sold around the world and, like any other product, the value is determined by supply and demand. For example, if the demand for the British pound grows in the United States of America, the value of this currency will grow against the US dollar. Nations may also want to have a fixed/pegged exchange rate against various nations' currencies to avoid undesirable outcomes happening with the demand and supply of their own currency and possibly to stabilise their economy as a result.

Exchange rates are calculated by market forces of supply and demand with various factors that may have an influence, which could include inflation rates, interest rates, trade balance between exports and imports, general state of the economy, political stability, internal harmony of the nation, and quality of governance. So, as you can see, there are many economic factors that influence a nation's international exchange rate.

A good reason to keep an eye on exchange rates, as they vary due to economic market influences, is because holiday destinations can be very good value if their currency is low against your own nation's currency. Also, if you plan to relocate to another country, you will want to make sure you get the best value for your own currency when converting to your new nation's currency. For example, when I first relocated to England, I could exchange approximately AUD $2.10 per £1, and then post-Brexit it dropped to approximately AUD $1.60 per £1.

CURRENCY IS CONTINUALLY BOUGHT AND SOLD AROUND WORLD AND, LIKE ANY OTHER PRODUCT, THE VALUE IS DETERMINED BY SUPPLY AND DEMAND

QUICK LESSONS ON GENERAL LIFE SKILLS

QUICK LESSON 42: The importance of emotional intelligence

When I was at school in Australia, there was a great emphasis on achieving good grades and a high TER (Tertiary Entrance Rank) score in year 12, which is the final year of high school. This was because you must achieve a certain TER to gain entry on to university courses. To me, the TER was an indication on your 'book smart' skills achieved at school and has no real bearing on your personality and what we call emotional intelligence, which in my opinion is what helps you with most jobs in the real world. I say most jobs because if you are a rocket scientist, for example, then I am sure you need a good IQ (intelligence quotient) and be exceptional in maths and science. However, most jobs in the real world are not like this.

My understanding of emotional intelligence is your ability to manage your own emotions and the emotions of others. This type of intelligence is very helpful in being able to understand people and how they work, which I think is a better skill in the real world than being able to solve calculus equations. Make sense? There are a lot of people I went to school with who achieved higher TER scores than I did, but they have not been as successful in their professional lives. I believe this is because they are not good with people or do not have high emotional intelligence.

Emotional intelligence is important in the business world as all businesses are essentially people and how they work together. By better understanding our emotions and others, we are then able to communicate our feelings in a more constructive way. We can then also be better at relating to others we work with by understanding their own needs and feelings. This leads to stronger and more fulfilling relationships. I believe there has been a lot of research that shows EQ (emotional intelligence) is more important in the business world than IQ, and it is better at predicting the quality of relationships and overall success of individuals.

For some people, emotional intelligence comes naturally; you will notice that some are just better at dealing with people than others. There are many ways you can learn emotional intelligence skills to increase your success in the real world, which should be further researched.

> **EMOTIONAL INTELLIGENCE IS IMPORTANT IN THE BUSINESS WORLD AS ALL BUSINESSES ARE ESSENTIALLY PEOPLE AND HOW THEY WORK TOGETHER**

QUICK LESSON 43: Have a plan and set goals

I believe that you should always have a plan in life and always set goals for both the short term and long term. Having goals and a general plan can give you structure. This will help with what you do, how you do it, where you are going and generally how you go about your life. Without plans and goals, you could just be ambling along without a real purpose. I prefer to have goals that are realistic and achievable as well as others which might be more of a dream than achievable – but sometimes you will have to dream big to achieve big! Also, it is good to have a plan just to remind yourself what you are trying to achieve when life is hectic and you might question what you are doing and where you are heading.

Once you have a plan and set your goals, you will need to put steps into place to achieve these. As an example, if your plan/goal is to buy a house in 18 months but you have minimal savings for a deposit, you should put together an action plan to save enough money. If your goal is to be promoted, you will have to work out what you need to do to achieve this. You could even sit down with your manager and document what is required for this to happen. Remember to be open to any type of feedback you might receive as a result.

Make sure that you write down your goals, set a reasonable time frame and then make sure you assess where you are partway through. You could set goals that are to be achieved in six months, but just make sure you assess the steps you have taken at the two-month and four-month intervals to ensure you are on track. Remember, goals and plans can change over time, which is a part of life, so just adapt to these changes and reassess your plan when this happens.

> **ONCE YOU HAVE A PLAN AND SET YOUR GOALS, YOU WILL NEED TO PUT STEPS INTO PLACE TO ACHIEVE THESE**

QUICK LESSON 44: Dating and relationships

Now, this topic can be very difficult for men and women of all ages. Basically, men can confuse women and women can confuse men, especially throughout our teenage years and early twenties. Dating and relationships was not really taught to me at school, but this subject would be very hard to teach because there is certainly no right or wrong way to approach it. There are numerous psychologists who have devoted their lives to this topic and give relationship advice along with lots of varying guidance and opinion online.

The best neutral advice I can give for both men and women is to understand that generally us humans seem to run away from what chases us. We enjoy a challenge, but we do not like desperate and clingy people. You can use this mindset to think about how you should approach dating and relationships. The more desperate and needy men look to women, the less attractive they could be, and vice versa. Have you ever noticed how confident and successful men who barely try seem to do the best as women appear to be naturally attracted to them? This could be because they have attractive features to women that are over and above looks. The same could be said about women, as there are always girls who are clingy and needy that can end up having a difficult time in the dating world.

Yes, being good-looking has its advantages; however, this will only get you so far. As the dating world continually changes, with dating apps such as Tinder, the way people meet a potential partner is changing from the previous traditional ways. You should always remember that your face-to-face personality is always going to be your best asset in the dating world and will keep you in a relationship. Having a good sense of humour will always separate you from the crowd and make you fun to be around. Further to this, I suggest you check online for more detailed advice. Just be careful about what you believe as there is both good and bad information out there.

> **WE ENJOY A CHALLENGE, BUT WE DO NOT LIKE DESPERATE AND CLINGY PEOPLE**

QUICK LESSON 45: The importance of sport

Apart from the obvious benefits of sport such as enjoyment and fitness, others come in handy in the real world. These relate to the lessons 'The benefits of networking' and 'The importance of being a team player' we have already discussed in this book.

If you play a sport, numerous sports or even become involved with a sports club, you are automatically part of a large network. There are many benefits of being a part of this network, yet a lot of the time the people involved don't even realise. For example, if you ever start your own business such as a gardener or greenskeeper, I am sure you would get many customers from that sports club alone. Vice versa if you ever needed a trustworthy gardener who could offer good or even discounted rates, as you could of course use your connections from the sports team/club you are involved with.

Unless you are playing an individual sport such as tennis or golf, you are generally playing within a team environment where everyone must work together for a common goal, which is usually for winning success, and you are learning the skill of working in a team just by being involved. This can then help you to be a strong team member in the real world, such as being part of a team in the workplace. A lot of people don't realise but if you play a sport from a young age and are taught to be a team player, this skill can subconsciously stay with you for the rest of your life.

I believe that being involved in a sporting team/club can be one of the best networks to be a part of, as you can build relationships on personal and emotional levels as well as learning to be a team player.

> **IF YOU PLAY A SPORT, NUMEROUS SPORTS OR EVEN BECOME INVOLVED WITH A SPORTS CLUB, YOU ARE AUTOMATICALLY PART OF A LARGE NETWORK**

QUICK LESSON 46: The importance of travel

I did not leave my home country of Australia or even own a passport until I was 20 years old. I love Australia and I miss my country of origin, but I believe travelling and experiencing everything the world has to offer is by far the best thing anyone can do with their life. In my opinion, every part of travelling is part of the experience and story associated, whether good or bad, and it is very unlikely that you will ever regret travelling.

I have read numerous articles/surveys about happiness/well-being and the underlying theme seems to be that people gain more happiness from experiences in life than material possessions. I can completely relate to this. Although I haven't been lucky enough to have a gap year, I do believe I have travelled as much as I can while having a balanced life with work commitments. I feel that I am very lucky to have lived in three countries, which are all very different in their own right even though they are all English-speaking nations. I left a good, stable job in Adelaide to experience the UK and Europe with no job lined up afterwards. You might think this was a bit of a risk, but it was a risk that enabled me to experience more of the world. Sometimes you might have to escape your comfort zone to get more out of life by travelling.

To me, the experiences associated with travel will stay with you for the rest of your life. Travelling has never been as easy and affordable as it is right now. Flights around the world are getting quicker and more efficient as time goes by. Also, because of the internet, you can always shop around for the cheapest airline and travel route associated.

So, save your money and research the travel experiences you would like the most, and then go and travel the world!

> **THE UNDERLYING THEME SEEMS TO BE THAT PEOPLE GAIN MORE HAPPINESS FROM EXPERIENCES IN LIFE THAN MATERIAL POSSESSIONS**

QUICK LESSON 47: The importance of insurance

Insurance is an arrangement where a company or state will undertake to guarantee a monetary compensation for a loss, damage, sickness or death after receiving a payment on an incremental basis premium in return. I believe insurance is very important throughout your life as it protects you from a large financial loss. This could be due to an emergency, accident, sickness or an unforeseen circumstance that occurs.

The reason I believe insurance is so important in the real world is because shit happens and shit can happen at any time. There are car accidents on the road all the time, and many of these accidents are by good, competent drivers and are therefore unforeseen.

Sickness/illness can happen at any time to any person on the planet and possibly with no real warning. Injuries can happen in sport at any time to any person and can vary in nature. You should always protect yourself and family members for when shit happens.

There are various different types of insurance, some of which I believe to be more important than others. There is private insurance and state or government funded insurance. For example, in the United Kingdom there is the NHS, which is a healthcare service fully funded by the government. Whereas in Australia there is Medicare, which is a healthcare service that part funds the health sector. My opinion is that private health insurance is more important for healthcare protection in Australia than in the UK for that reason. I injured my knee badly in both Australia and the UK, but I was lucky to have insurance in Australia and that the NHS was in place in the UK so I could have the corrective surgeries required.

Here is a list of insurance items I believe you should take out as a minimum:

1. Car insurance – To protect yourself and other drivers/vehicles on the road in the event of a car accident.

2. Health Insurance – To protect yourself from expenses incurred due to sickness, illness and injuries.

3. House and contents insurance – To ensure you receive compensation from burglaries and accidental damage to your property and belongings.

4. Travel insurance – This is very important protection for any accidents and emergencies that could happen while you are away/abroad.

5. Life insurance – To protect your partner and family in the event of death.

When looking to obtain any type of insurance, make sure you shop around and negotiate to get the best deal. Insurance companies will generally move on price to get you on board as a customer. As an example, when I first moved to the UK from Australia I was receiving quotations of approximately £5,000 a year for car insurance purely because I had an international driver's licence (even driving conditions are very similar in both countries), but eventually I agreed a fee of approximately £1,000 a year by shopping around.

THE REASON I BELIEVE INSURANCE IS SO IMPORTANT IN THE REAL WORLD IS BECAUSE SHIT HAPPENS AND SHIT CAN HAPPEN AT ANY TIME

QUICK LESSON 48: The importance of family

As time goes on, I have also realised how important family is. Specifically my parents because at the end of the day your parents may be the only people in the world who will literally stand by your side and support you through anything (or at least most things in life). For this reason, you should always look after your parents and treat them well. Also, you never really know how long members of your family will be around for, so you should always enjoy the time you have with them as best as you possibly can.

When I was younger in my teenage years, I found a lot of what my parents said to me as being annoying and it felt as though they were always nagging. But, as you get older, you start to realise a lot of what they are telling you has some sort of meaning as they have experienced a lot more in life than you have at that age. You should always listen to your parents, or at least take in certain aspects of what they are saying, and learn from what they say – instead of being like most teenagers and dismissing everything they say!

My suggestion is to keep in contact with family members as best you can no matter what the circumstances. It has never been easier to keep in contact by using Skype/smartphones/social media. Even though I live a long way away from my parents, I always make sure we talk regularly, which is usually through a Skype video call every couple of weeks on a Sunday. A lot of people fall out and fight with family members. If this does happen, why not be the one to reconcile the situation and forgive your family for whatever has happened. You might regret it later if you don't and then lose contact over something that could have been forgiven and forgotten.

> **YOUR PARENTS MAY BE THE ONLY PEOPLE IN THE WORLD WHO WILL LITERALLY STAND BY YOUR SIDE AND SUPPORT YOU THROUGH ANYTHING (OR AT LEAST MOST THINGS IN LIFE)**

QUICK LESSON 49: Grades in school aren't 'that' important

I believe the education system I experienced in South Australia was very much focused around what I would call 'book smarts'. The final marks/grades you received in the final year of secondary schooling (year 12) dictated pretty much all the university courses you could gain entry to the following year (apart from medicine, which I believe included an interview and a psychiatric assessment as well). Grades received from my high school very much reflected people's IQ, or what I call book smarts, and really did not consider people's emotional intelligence (as per Quick Lesson 42), which I believe is generally more important in the real world we live in.

Because of the reasons mentioned above, I believe that grades from school are not really *that* important. Don't get me wrong, getting good grades in school is great and of course it can help you in life, but there is a lot more to it than that and your life is not over if you achieve poor grades in school. Life skills and lessons, as included within this book, really help you to be successful in many aspects of life.

There are many examples of very highly successful people, specifically in business, who either dropped out of school early or did not do well at school. I suggest you do a bit of research on these success stories for inspiration. The grades I received in school were not as good as they could have been. This resulted in me getting into my second preference course selection at university, which really worked out to be the best as I could have ended up being an architect (apologies to the architects out there, but you are different people that I have worked alongside for years!). Either way, your parents might not like me saying this, but don't stress (too much) if you don't get the school grades you are after. There are many other opportunities in life to achieve your goals/dreams by learning other various skills.

GRADES RECEIVED FROM MY HIGH SCHOOL VERY MUCH REFLECTED PEOPLE'S IQ, OR WHAT I CALL BOOK SMARTS, AND REALLY DID NOT CONSIDER PEOPLE'S EMOTIONAL INTELLIGENCE (AS PER QUICK LESSON 42), WHICH I BELIEVE IS GENERALLY MORE IMPORTANT IN THE REAL WORLD WE LIVE IN

QUICK LESSON 50: The positives and negatives of alcohol consumption

I enjoy a drink and have always enjoyed drinking alcohol in various quantities since my late teenage years. Like most things, there are positives and negatives associated with the consumption of the drug called alcohol. You must also understand that different people with differing genetic make-ups will handle and react to alcohol in different ways, so you need to make your own choice about alcohol consumption and whether this provides you with more positives than negatives in your life.

I believe the biggest positive aspect alcohol has on most people and society as a whole is the networking and social interaction that is enhanced through alcohol consumption. Let's face it, responsible alcohol consumption makes us more sociable and assists us in communicating with people in one way or another. A lot of great friendships and relationships flourish with the addition of alcohol to the social interactions that take place because it can help you to relax and become livelier.

The moderate or, what I would say, the responsible use of alcohol can also help in business networking scenarios for the same reasons mentioned above, which is good for the economy as it creates a lot of jobs and economic growth in the entertainment, retail, catering and services sectors. Many business deals all over the world take place over a drink. This positive social and networking effect of alcohol should never be forgotten when looking at the negatives of alcohol consumption.

There are of course consequences due to excessive or irresponsible consumption. Firstly, there are many negative impacts to your health as a result of alcohol consumption, which can easily be researched for more detail. Alcohol can have very harmful effects on unborn babies during pregnancy and should really be avoided completely during this time. Alcohol consumption, especially when irresponsible, can contribute to aggression and violent acts from people.

I read that around 40% of the people who reported incidents from aggression were as a direct result of alcohol consumption. Police spend a fair percentage of their time on cases involving excessive drinking. However, it is worth noting that many people do not get aggressive through alcohol consumption. It is usually those who already have these tendencies that become more aggressive after drinking alcohol.

> **MANY BUSINESS DEALS ALL OVER THE WORLD TAKE PLACE OVER A DRINK. THIS POSITIVE SOCIAL AND NETWORKING EFFECT OF ALCOHOL SHOULD NEVER BE FORGOTTEN WHEN LOOKING AT THE NEGATIVES OF ALCOHOL CONSUMPTION**

QUICK LESSON 51: The importance of learning about 'irrelevant' information at school

I have already mentioned that there is a lot of possibly irrelevant information that we learn throughout our years at school. This is not necessarily a waste of time because school teaches us many necessary skills required when you enter the real world.

I believe the main advantage is learning how to learn, which of course helps us to prepare for many of the skills required after education. Throughout our lives we are always learning new information, nearly on a daily basis. We should never stop wanting to learn and develop new skills, even if they are not specifically taught at school. We are taught to learn new information and skills on a continual basis and over many years; this is great preparation for the years ahead.

At school, you will also learn the skills of responsibility and independence as the years go on. Generally, before you start school, we rely predominantly on our parents for everything we need. However, at school it becomes our own responsibility to complete the necessary work and assignments that are required as part of any course. We must make sure that we study the topics we are working on to prepare for tests and exams. We must at times prepare for oral presentations that are to be completed in front of an audience. All of these skills are then required for the real world after our educational studies.

I am also a strong believer that if you can learn to be independent and take responsibility for yourself at school, without relying too much on your parents and teachers, then this will hold you in good stead for the rest of your life. If you have always relied on others, such as your parents or teachers to get through life, how can you ever survive on your own when you leave school/university?

> **AT SCHOOL, YOU WILL ALSO LEARN THE SKILLS OF RESPONSIBILITY AND INDEPENDENCE AS THE YEARS GO ON**

QUICK LESSONS ON LIFE SKILLS FOR YOURSELF

QUICK LESSON 52: Always be personable with people

There are some people who are naturally good at communicating with others, this can also be known in the real world as 'street smarts'. These people are also generally successful in their professional and business lives. I believe that anyone can be good at communicating by being personable with all people in all aspects of life.

This is a lesson I did not learn until my first real-world job as a project manager assistant while still studying at university and when I was very close to losing my job. At this age, I seemed to think that I knew more/better than my colleagues, many of which had a lot more experience within the industry than I did. This was obviously not the case, and it took a candid conversation with my boss for me to realise that I needed to be more personable with my co-workers to keep my job and also to get the desired results from colleagues.

To have positive relationships, you should always try to understand the perspectives of others and why they behave the way they do. If you are open and listen to the opinions of others, rather than being narrow-minded or unreceptive, then of course they may be open and listen to you, which is just basic human nature. If you are personable with the people you work with, they should be personable with you and you can work together to achieve the desired results. I always used to have trouble working with architects on building projects. One day I worked out that once I opened up my mind, tried to understand their perspective and worked reasonably with them, they started to work reasonably with me in return.

IF YOU ARE PERSONABLE WITH THE PEOPLE YOU WORK WITH, THEY SHOULD BE PERSONABLE WITH YOU AND YOU CAN WORK TOGETHER TO ACHIEVE THE DESIRED RESULTS

QUICK LESSON 53: Have multiple income streams

This is something I am yet to master; however, I believe that one of the best ways to earn more money is to have multiple income streams. I read recently from a study carried out that a large percentage of self-made millionaires generate multiple streams of income.

There are many ways to generate multiple income streams, but working two jobs, seven days a week, is probably not the best way to do this as you are simply trading your time for money. My plan is to have three streams of income over the next couple of years:

1. Base working salary

2. Owning rental properties

3. Writing books (thanks for your assistance!)

I believe the easiest form of income outside your Monday-to-Friday job is to own rental properties, especially in areas with good rental yields, i.e. those which are generating income because the rental payments are higher than the mortgage loan repayments for the property. If there is also good capital growth in these areas, properties can make you money every month as well as being a good long-term investment. Beware that there is of course the risk of these properties going down in value during poor economic conditions, but you can keep the properties until the market improves if you are still generating a good rental return. The other benefit to owning rental properties is they will take up very little of your time once you have purchased the property and tenants are living there, so it shouldn't interfere too much with your work-life balance compared to, for example, having a second job!

Other forms of income could include stock market investments or part-ownership of a business. From the study I discussed earlier, three income streams was the magic number for the majority of self-made millionaires: 65% had three or more streams, 45% had four or more streams and 29% had five or more streams.

ONE OF THE BEST WAYS TO EARN MORE MONEY IS TO HAVE MULTIPLE INCOME STREAMS

QUICK LESSON 54: The importance of time management

We live in a world of time precision in various aspects of life. In the real world, it becomes even more important to effectively manage your own time. Depending on your profession/career path, part of your role may involve managing people and their time. If you cannot manage your own time, how will you effectively manage other people's time?

I always like to make sure that I am never late for anything in my professional and personal life (if possible), and I always wish everyone else I know would do the same. Obviously, there are times when you cannot help being late, for example if a train breaks down on your journey, but mostly your arrival time is within your control. If you are constantly late getting to work/school/university in the morning due to bad traffic, then you will probably need to look at leaving home earlier to give yourself enough time.

In this modern age we are living in, we have tools and devices available at all times to help us manage our time. You should use these devices and specifically a calendar, whether this is on a computer or phone, as an electronic calendar is the best way to schedule and manage your time. Always be realistic about what you can achieve in your calendar. If you genuinely can't make a meeting due to previously agreed commitments, suggest an alternative time and ensure enough reasonable time is allocated for the meeting you are arranging. There is no point in overcommitting yourself as you could end up letting other people down.

Please also remember that how you manage your time will affect other people in your life. If you are late for a meeting, this may affect other people's schedules at the meeting. If you are late to a family gathering, this may affect your family. I am a strong believer that you should never, if at all possible, be late to anything that involves other people, as this is like saying that you feel your time is more important than theirs.

IF YOU CANNOT MANAGE YOUR OWN TIME, HOW WILL YOU EFFECTIVELY MANAGE OTHER PEOPLE'S TIME?

QUICK LESSON 55: The importance of life balance

I am a big believer in having a balanced life because this can help in all aspects of your life. Have you ever noticed that you feel so much better and more fulfilled if you have a couple of drinks to celebrate working hard for something than if you do nothing and then have a couple of drinks? If the weather has been average, you seem to appreciate the sunny days a lot more. If you live in a sunny country, you seem to take that for granted because it is normal (like my former life living in Australia!). If you do too much of one thing and don't balance it out with other aspects of life, it can really wear you down. My suggestion is to find the right balance to get the most enjoyment and satisfaction out of life.

Did you ever think that with good planning and good money management you would be able to do most of the things you want to do if you don't overindulge? If you manage your money well, you will be able to travel the world, buy a house, buy a car, etc. However, if you do too much of one thing, it might affect other things you could do. For example, if you travel a lot and go to expensive countries, you might not be able to buy a nice house. If you buy a house that is too expensive for what you can afford to have a balanced life, you may not be able to travel/go on holidays. In my opinion, this would result in an unbalanced lifestyle.

How balanced your life is can also be a personal preference. So, if all you want to do is travel the world and you're not interested in owning a house, then do it. If you want to have a balanced life, make sure you do not overindulge in one aspect and then be disappointed if another aspect of your life suffers.

Make a list of what you like to do/want to achieve and start planning how to balance your life. Personally, I like working hard, travelling, socialising, sports, and I want to own various properties and have children (sometime!). So I will try to balance out this lifestyle as best I can through planning and money management.

> **IF YOU WANT TO HAVE A BALANCED LIFE, MAKE SURE YOU DO NOT OVERINDULGE IN ONE ASPECT AND THEN BE DISAPPOINTED IF ANOTHER ASPECT OF YOUR LIFE SUFFERS**

QUICK LESSON 56: The importance of to-do lists

List writing is a personal skill of mine I wish I'd used effectively from a younger age and throughout my schooling life. We all have so much information stored inside our head that I do not believe we should always rely on our brain's memory to remember everything we need to. We can write it all down in the form of a to-do list.

You can become more productive by completing items on a list and you could be more efficient if you finish the items on the list quickly. Employers look for these positive traits from job applicants/potential employees.

Lists can give structure to what you need and want to do. They can take many forms, such as a shopping list, work action list, bucket list, travel list, goal list and a house to-do list. This skill is not for everyone. But if you function like me, you should write lists and then action the items, which should give you a sense of satisfaction once the tasks have been completed.

Lists can be effective for time management as they consolidate your tasks in one place. You can then prioritise and make sure the important tasks are completed first. I am a strong believer that to-do lists should always be realistic and achievable. When writing a daily list of tasks at work, make sure the items are achievable during that day. Otherwise, you may be burning the midnight oil to complete all the tasks or you will simply ignore the list because it is not achievable.

In the spirit of list writing, here is my list of the top five benefits of writing a to-do list:

1. A to-do list will remind you what you need to complete so you won't forget

2. A to-do list can increase your individual productivity

3. A to-do list is helpful with time management

4. A to-do list can help prioritise tasks

5. A to-do list can give you satisfaction when completing tasks

This book is a list of quick lessons for the real world so you can prioritise and then study further in your own life!

LISTS CAN BE EFFECTIVE FOR TIME MANAGEMENT AS THEY CONSOLIDATE YOUR TASKS IN ONE PLACE

QUICK LESSON 57: Prioritising tasks

After learning about the importance of lists in Quick Lesson 56, a key skill that can separate you from many other people in the business world is the ability to analyse and rank the tasks from your lists in order of importance.

My advice when you have a list of tasks and activities in place is to go through and realistically write down how long you estimate each will take along with the date they are required to be completed. If you're not sure of the time frame, it would be worth consulting with your boss/manager as well as any necessary work colleagues. Once you have completed this activity, you can then rank your action list in preference order. You can also use your calendar to allocate approximate time slots for when each of the activities can be finished. Your calendar is one of the best time management tools you can use very easily.

You might find that you will have to either cancel or reschedule meetings in your calendar to complete the work required. In this case, you should analyse whether the meetings are more important or the tasks you are required to complete.

Another piece of advice I have learnt over the past few years is learning to say no to additional work or projects that may be offered to you. As you progress in your career, there will be an influx of opportunities presented that will have some impact on your available time. Make sure you prioritise what is the most important to you (and of course the business by discussing with your boss/manager) and decline others that are not critical/time dependant.

Referring to work-life balance, as discussed in Quick Lesson 55, it will be very difficult to achieve a good life balance if you are taking on too many tasks and a lot of additional work that is not adding to your career progression or valuable to the business you are working in. If you are struggling with your life balance and workload, which isn't any different to your work colleagues, you might have to look at how you are managing your time as mentioned in Quick Lesson 54.

> **A KEY SKILL THAT CAN SEPARATE YOU FROM MANY OTHER PEOPLE IN THE BUSINESS WORLD IS THE ABILITY TO ANALYSE AND RANK THE TASKS FROM YOUR LISTS IN ORDER OF IMPORTANCE**

QUICK LESSON 58: The importance of self-acceptance

I feel this is a very important lesson that I personally was not taught by anyone. You are going to live with yourself for every second of every minute of every day of your life. So, why not accept who you are and get on with it? So many people worry about who they are and how they look, which ultimately holds them back from many possibilities in life.

Accept the genetic hand you have been dealt and get on with living your life. You should only work on the things that are within your reasonable control. If there are certain aspects of your personality that you do not like, you can always work on these attributes through learnt skills. I have completed a Diploma of Management and Leadership, which taught me a lot of skills for working with people to build relationships. I wouldn't say this skill came naturally to my personality; however, I was able to work and develop these skills over time. Everyone can work on their own personality.

Unless you have a lot of spare money, you cannot largely change the way you look. So accept this and get on with your life – don't let this hold you back. If you let these feelings about your appearance get to you, it can continually affect your life and the quality of life you are living.

Self-acceptance of who you are is a real skill that will go a long way to being successful in the real world, so accept yourself and work on what you can to achieve your goals.

> **UNLESS YOU HAVE A LOT OF SPARE MONEY, YOU CANNOT LARGELY CHANGE THE WAY YOU LOOK. SO ACCEPT THIS AND GET ON WITH YOUR LIFE – DON'T LET THIS HOLD YOU BACK**

QUICK LESSON 59: The importance of getting out of your comfort zone

I believe we are wired as humans to get comfortable and stay comfortable. This can include physical, psychological and emotional comfort. A common trait of wealthy and very successful people is being comfortable by being uncomfortable. These people know that becoming rich or really successful, in any aspect of life, isn't easy and that being comfortable could be detrimental to achieving success. If you can learn to be comfortable by working in a world of mayhem, which can include a lot of uncertainty/risk, and if you can develop a mental toughness to be able to sustain some hardship and pain, then you could come out the other side more successful.

I had a good standard of life growing up in Adelaide in Australia, which is what I would have called my comfort zone, but I was very much in the bubble of this city that was so familiar to me. I had a good steady project management job, but I always felt that I needed to experience more out of life. I had never been to the UK or travelled around Europe, so I decided to quit my job and move overseas to experience travelling and working abroad. This was something my mother could not understand: why take the risk of leaving a good job and have the uncertainty of trying to find your way in a new country. After a few months of travelling, I moved into a place just outside Manchester and received a job offer within three days. I now earn comparably more money and work on much bigger projects than I ever would have in Adelaide. Also, I met my future wife in Manchester and travelled around a lot of Europe. I am very happy I made this decision, even though I really miss my home country.

Getting out of your comfort zone and taking some risks can lead to amazing things. Not many people become wealthy or truly successful by staying in the same place and working in the same job. If you read and research autobiographies of numerous successful people, you might see a trend where most took large risks at certain points in their life, which ended up paying dividends in the future.

GETTING OUT OF YOUR COMFORT ZONE AND TAKING SOME RISKS CAN LEAD TO AMAZING THINGS

QUICK LESSON 60: Learning from failure

I am a strong believer that failing at anything can be the first step to succeeding at anything. This might read like an unusual statement, but sometimes we can learn more from our failures than from our successes. There is possibly a misguided concept around the world that failure is bad, which might be true at the time it takes place or even in the short term. However, failures can be one of the real reasons for success in the long term. You just need to approach failures in the right way. There is a famous quote from former NBA basketballer Michael Jordan that I really like: 'I've missed more than 9000 shots in my career. I've lost almost 300 games. 26 times, I've been trusted to take the game winning shot and missed. I've failed over and over again in my life. And that is why I succeed.'

Failures happen in all aspects of life and sometimes they are completely unavoidable. When failings take place, it is best to learn from them and not play the blame game. A lot of people seem to think that if someone is not blamed for a failing or a mistake they will not learn from it. The contractor I worked for in the construction industry in Australia placed a very high importance on safety in the construction industry. At one point in time, senior management used to play the blame game on employees if there was a safety incident rather than working with the staff to learn from the mistake, which ended up becoming counterproductive and the number of safety incidents did not seem to improve. Then one day, this changed and fewer incidents took place because senior management decided not to blame employees for any incidents. This brought trust back into the organisation and employees started learning from the mistakes.

I believe a safe work environment is the best way to learn from failures. I am sure that one of the main reasons Michael Jordan became so successful was because he worked within a team and family that had confidence in him to succeed. Once the company I worked for decided to make a safe working environment rather than play the blame game, people started to learn from the failings to create a successful environment.

> **WHEN FAILINGS TAKE PLACE, IT IS BEST TO LEARN FROM THEM AND NOT PLAY THE BLAME GAME**

QUICK LESSON 61: Surround yourself with positive, like-minded people

I have read before that a common attribute of very wealthy people is that they surround themselves with positive people and stay away from those who surround themselves with negativity. In short, positive people are successful. You can see this in all facets of life. The idea is to surround yourself with the types of people who share your vision and have a positive mindset. This is because the alignment of several positive-minded people is going to be even more powerful and effective than that of one. We also end up becoming like the people we associate with, so you could be successful if you surround yourself with positive and like-minded people.

To a certain extent, it is human nature to act negatively and complain. Some people complain all the time and end up having a negative nature as a result, which can stop them succeeding in many aspects of life as well as this impacting on those around them. Most people will complain about something from time to time. However, I try to be positive and upbeat about life, but I still end up complaining sometimes. For example, as an Australian living in the United Kingdom, I naturally end up complaining about the weather even though there is no real benefit to this. Sometimes it is a good way to create small talk with other Australians living in the UK, but there is no real benefit because I can't change the weather and it's my choice to live here. This negative thought pattern about the weather can affect my mood, mindset and even body language throughout the day.

On the sporting field, is there any real benefit in complaining to a referee/umpire? No. If anything, complaining will make them remember you and it could work against you for other decisions throughout the game/season ahead. My suggestion is to focus on what you can control in your own game rather than worrying about refereeing decisions that may ultimately affect your performance.

In business, will complaining about your allocated tasks and work colleagues help your career development? Probably not. If you get on with the tasks requested, you could be respected for this. If you work well with difficult work colleagues, you could stand head and shoulders above everyone else.

> **POSITIVE PEOPLE ARE SUCCESSFUL. YOU CAN SEE THIS IN ALL FACETS OF LIFE. THE IDEA IS TO SURROUND YOURSELF WITH THE TYPES OF PEOPLE WHO SHARE YOUR VISION AND HAVE A POSITIVE MINDSET**

QUICK LESSON 62: Nothing good happens after 2 a.m.

This is a lesson I have learnt from experience in my life and it is discussed on one of my favourite TV shows *How I Met Your Mother*. Looking back over my 30 years of life (of what I can remember anyway), I can't remember anything good that happened after 2 a.m. or that there was any real benefit from being out past 2 a.m. apart from staying with friends on a night out. I'm not saying abandon your friends and loved ones after this time just because nothing good happens. And, of course, use a bit of common sense in relation to any situation you are in!

Usually after this time, your general ability to make good decisions has dropped dramatically. This is because you are either too drunk or too tired to make good decisions.

The best advice I can give when faced with a life decision or choice that could be made after 2 a.m., it's probably best to leave it until the next day when you should be in the correct frame of mind. As an example, if your ex-girlfriend/ex-boyfriend from a previous poor/abusive relationship is messaging you for a catch-up after 2 a.m., it is probably best to ignore this (even if at the time you really miss them) and have a think about the best decision to make the next day (or at least after a good amount of sleep).

From my experience, we tend to make incorrect, irrational decisions after 2 a.m., so we are best avoiding making choices we will probably regret until we can think about things more coherently and logically.

> **USUALLY AFTER THIS TIME, YOUR GENERAL ABILITY TO MAKE GOOD DECISIONS HAS DROPPED DRAMATICALLY. THIS IS BECAUSE YOU ARE EITHER TOO DRUNK OR TOO TIRED TO MAKE GOOD DECISIONS**

Remember nothing (generally) good happens after 2 a.m.

QUICK LESSON 63: First aid

A few years ago when I was living in Adelaide while at university, I was travelling on the tram one day and someone collapsed right next to me. At the time, I had never carried out any first aid and I did not know how to react to the situation, apart from the basics of calling an ambulance (which is actually one of the key responses as a first-aider). No one around me knew how to conduct any first-aid treatment either, so this person lay there unassisted until an ambulance arrived. Luckily, this person regained consciousness and survived the collapse, but I felt very shaken up and helpless because of the situation that had occurred.

I now know after taking a first-aid course that this person should have been moved into a recovery position (rather than lying on their back as they were), their airways should have been checked to ensure they were cleared, I should have checked for breathing and then commenced CPR if needed until the ambulance arrived.

The point to this story is that you never know when you could be required to step in and provide first aid to someone who requires assistance to hopefully save their life.

A first-aid course usually takes about one day every few years and can give you the basic skills and knowledge to possibly save someone's life in the future. I believe first-aid lessons should be a part of every school curriculum around the world for this reason. Just think about how good you would feel if you ever saved someone's life because of your first-aid skills.

Make sure you book into a first-aid course, and then undertake refresher courses to keep up to date with the training that is being provided.

> **JUST THINK ABOUT HOW GOOD YOU WOULD FEEL IF YOU EVER SAVED SOMEONE'S LIFE BECAUSE OF YOUR FIRST-AID SKILLS**

QUICK LESSON 64: Always look after your belongings

As per Quick Lesson 46, travelling around the world is one of the best things we can do in our life; however, any trip could turn into a potential disaster if we were to lose any of our essential or valuable personal belongings.

While recently on a trip to Europe with my parents, we arrived in Paris and sat outside at a café for lunch with our luggage bags. Within about 15 minutes my mum's backpack, which was right next to her at the time, was stolen. Her passport, wallet and phone were inside the bag. Luckily, the waiter at the café was on the case. He chased down the thief, who was then surrounded by four undercover police and six men from the French military within seconds (it was the weekend before the presidential election, so there was a huge amount of police/military presence in the city at the time!), and the bag was returned.

Just think how awful this would have been for my mother if those belongings were gone for good. Imagine being in a foreign country with no form of identity, no passport, and no cash or bank/credit cards. Thieves are everywhere, especially cities. They are very good at what they do and have usually gone before you've even realised what they've done.

Make sure your bags are on you or in front of you, and constantly check your pockets to protect your valuables, especially when you are travelling to foreign places.

IMAGINE BEING IN A FOREIGN COUNTRY WITH NO FORM IDENTITY, NO PASSPORT, AND NO CASH OR BANK/CREDIT CARDS

QUICK LESSON 65: Importance of putting life into perspective sometimes

Sometimes you should put life into perspective. Very recently, I went on a trip to Amiens in France (for ANZAC day) and Berlin in Germany. On this trip I learnt a lot about some dark modern history in relation to what had taken place in World War I on the Western Front and also in World War II under the Nazi regime in Europe. Soon after this trip, I rocked into work on a Monday morning at the construction site where I am working in Manchester and found out that a dead body had been discovered on-site. This turned out to be a 19-year-old man who had broken in over the weekend and ended up falling from a great height to his death.

Around the same time as all of these events were taking place, I had been fairly stressed out at work as the project I was working on wasn't going as well as it should have and I was dealing with some fairly non-personable people. My stress at work and the reasoning behind this stress was very minor in the scheme of life when you consider the atrocities that some people endured through times of war, for example. This really put my life into perspective and got me thinking that I really need to take a step back sometimes to see the bigger picture.

Some things in life that we worry about and get stressed about are not really a big deal in the grand scheme of things. So we really need to just enjoy life while we can, especially with the prosperous and fairly peaceful world that we are living in at the moment.

MY STRESS AT WORK AND THE REASONING BEHIND THIS STRESS WAS VERY MINOR IN THE SCHEME OF LIFE WHEN YOU CONSIDER THE ATROCITIES THAT SOME PEOPLE ENDURED THROUGH TIMES OF WAR, FOR EXAMPLE

Sometimes, we just need to put our own lives into perspective and be grateful for what we have. Try not to overthink things and stress over fairly minor issues in the overall scheme of life.

I hope that you have enjoyed reading this book and that you have found the lessons informative and useful. Hopefully the quick lessons can be used as a foundation to learn about some certain topics in greater detail.

If you enjoyed this book, please take the time to share your thoughts and post a review on amazon. This would be very much appreciated as it will help others to make an informed decision before buying my book.

If you would like to get in touch with me please visit my Facebook page @quicklessonsfortherealworld and website on quicklessonsfortherealworld.wordpress.com.

Printed in Great Britain
by Amazon

82145694R00092